CRUISING TO GLORY

The Jon-Lewis Dickinson Story

PETER MANN BSC

Britain's Next
BESTSELLER

Published in 2018 by:
Britain's Next Bestseller
An imprint of Live It Ventures LTD
27 Old Gloucester Road
London.
WC1N 3AX
www.bnbsbooks.co.uk
@BNBSbooks
ISBN 978-1-910565-89-6
Cover designed by Rowland Kell
All images by SW
Sponsorship and logo courtesy of WM Utility Services LTD

This is my story, and it is dedicated to my loving family.

Foreword

RONNIE ROWE MBE

How can I start about Jon-Lewis Dickinson other than he gave me the time of my life, outside of my family, and a lot of people both know that and will agree with that statement but here's why he did it for me.

It's April 2010 and the day after Jon-Lewis won the Prizefighter tournament, defeating Leon Williams in the final.

I'll always remember that time when, after he'd won the tournament, we went to The Millhouse Pub for a meal.

The Prizefighter had been and gone rather quickly, it was all intense as you'd expect it to be and I said to him we'll go for a bit lunch and chill out.

There was this young lassie working that day, bless her, and when she'd got round to us paying the bill Jon-Lewis went to do it and I said no, I am, to which he insisted he was so I came back with "Jon, after the night you gave me last night, you've got to let me buy you dinner."

That lassie, her face just dropped, it was so funny at the time, I mean come on, here's Jon-Lewis, a six foot plus beast of a bloke, and there's me, a greying old fella – "Jon, after the night you gave last night," hilarious.

Whether at home, or abroad, anywhere, Jon was Jon and that's what made him, him.

Ireland, the times we had there were pretty special as well, although he could have killed me off a few times as well the daft bugger.

I've known Jon-Lewis Dickinson for a long time now, most of his life even, and it's an honour to be asked to provide the foreword for this, his life story.

Jon-Lewis, and his brother Travis, have both given me some great nights in the world of boxing, in the amateurs and professionals, and to have seen them grow into the men they have become has been a privilege.

We've has some really good times together, not only here in our native north-east but across the UK, and special trips away they were.

There's been times we can talk about, and probably some that we wouldn't dare mention, but they've all added to that relationship, that bond, the family in which we created, first at Birtley, then at Fighting Chance.

I've seen the boy that went in against Tony Bellew in the amateurs turn into a man, and that man, after a brief spell early doors in the pros under first, albeit briefly, Glenn McCrory and then Mickey Duncan, turn into a great fighter and champion, and now a loving family man.

When he came back to me, just before the Prizefighter, none of us knew, or could have predicted, what would happen but I for one wouldn't change any of it for the world.

We've been through a lot have myself, Jon, Travis, Lewis and others that have worked with Team Dickinson.

There's been highs, but also plenty of lows as well, a good few injuries, a couple of broken jaws, but we've seen it all off and it takes something, someone, quite special to go and achieve what he has done.

The injuries and losses made him the champion that he became, whether on Boxnation with Maloney, or on Sky Sports with the Hearn's.

After all, the amateur success combined with his creating history, becoming the only fighter to win the Prizefighter, (Northern) Area, English, and British titles, says a lot; he won the British, Lord Lonsdale belt, outright, against Neil Dawson, and took apart Stephen Simmons for the WBC International Silver, on two great nights at the Metro Radio Arena.

That, and who he is, a gentleman, makes Jon-Lewis Dickinson one of the good guys, and we love him for that.

Acknowledgments

Jon-Lewis Dickinson

Thank you's to my mum and dad for bringing me into this world and teaching me the values of life; to my grandad Jack for all he did in guiding me; to my brothers Mark and Travis, and sister Leanne; and to my wife Kate and son Joseph-Lewis – I love you all.

To those who have played a part in my boxing career, amateur and professional, be they management, coaching, opponents or sparring partners, you've all played a part in this story.

To Kellie Maloney (formerly Frank Maloney) for taking a chance on us Dickinson boys and guiding our careers in the pro ranks in the first part of my career, and to Lewis Pendleton in the second part.

Special mentions need to be to 'The Dish,' Ronnie Rowe, and Barrzy, Gary Barr, you're both amazing blokes and I suppose I love you equally...

And to anyone else I may have forgot, it's not intentional, but there'll be too many.

Hass Hass....

Acknowledgments

Peter Mann

I'd like to thank all those who gave their time, and thoughts, in putting this together, Jon's family and those connected to him through boxing.

Personally, the usual thanks to my mentor, Amanda McQueen, my adopted sister Chloe Chadwick for designing the covers of my books, and to David & Kelly McCaffrey and BNBS Publishers, without whom none of this would be possible.

And to Sharon Ward, without whom meeting, and interviewing, Kellie Maloney, would not have been possible.

DISCLAIMER – The information included in this book are correct to the best of mine and the subject's knowledge. Information has been gathered from the correct sources and is attributed to those persons where necessary.

Introduction

Boxing is a science, the study of a lifetime in which you may exhaust yourself but never your subject.

It is a contest, a duel, calling for skill and self-control.

It is a test of temper, a trial of honour, a revealer of character.

It affords the chance to play the man and act the gentleman.

It provides not only physical health but a natural force.

It includes companionship with friends and opportunities to excel in your chosen sport.

So, go for it, you would be champions and my you enjoy every moment of your sport.

But remember, we cannot all be champions.

"I used to love it when people bet on me to win fights and won some money. There was always, seemingly, big odds against me and it gave me a really good feeling. I've never gambled myself or even looked into it but a massive thanks to all that put their faith in me."
Jon-Lewis Dickinson; Cruising to Glory, 2018

ONE

Cruising To Glory

MY NAME IS Jon-Lewis Dickinson and this is my story.

It is the story of not only how I became the British cruiserweight champion, but, following gruelling contests against Shane McPhilbin, David Dolan and Mike Stafford and finally, in my home town of Newcastle-upon-Tyne, Neil Dawson, owned that Lonsdale belt outright.

Not only that, but because I am a history-maker, the only fighter to win, and in order I hasten to add, the Prizefighter (2010), Area (2011), English (2011) and British (2012-14) championships, I have what nobody can take away from me.

A lot has happened in my life that I am proud of personally, and professionally and it was to be against Neil Dawson, on that night in Newcastle, that my proudest moment as a professional boxer arrived.

At the Metro Radio Arena, on Saturday 29 March 2014 I stopped Rotherham's Neil Dawson in the tenth round of what was a gruelling, but exhilarating contest.

That night would prove to be Dawson's last professional outing, and not the first fighter who never appeared after facing me; I would go on to fight five more times though over the next couple of years, with mixed results.

But that one night in Newcastle, well two nights if you count the

1

Simmons fight, then I sure proved that I belonged in that title mix as we left it all in the ring, and I had that much needed, added incentive, on both occasions.

Incentive and not pressure, we Dickinson's don't do pressure.

I remember the week building up the Dawson fight quite well and our Travis, who was also a professional boxer, had knocked out Danny McIntosh in Sheffield's Ponds Forge Arena to claim the English light heavyweight strap and, if it wasn't for Bob Ajisafe's constant running away then our kid would have been a British champion as well, of that I'm sure.

Now that would have been something else, the Dickinson brothers both holding British titles in our respective divisions, but I guess it wasn't meant to be.

Anyway, after Travis had bagged himself the English title one of my nephews, there's a few, we have a big family, but yeah, our Jacob, he reached the semi-finals of the English 48kg Schoolboys Championships.

That night, which our Travis had in Sheffield, as well as the fight with Matty Clarkson, I was so very proud of him. He was brilliant, amazing, and put so much work, so much effort, into that and he was a different person, fighter. We could see that in him and that's what pushed me on to do the same against Dawson the following week, go out there, into that ring, and do what we did best, win.

I'd never thought beyond my winning that Lord Lonsdale belt outright, ask anyone and they'll say the same thing, I wanted that then hopefully go on to challenge for world honours.

I didn't want to miss my chance by looking elsewhere, going for something else, and it's every British boxers' dream, or at least it should be, to hold that British title, the Lord Lonsdale belt, outright.

That's when reality sets in, and that's what happened for me, waking up one morning and thinking, hold on, there's only a few days to go until the biggest fight night of my career and, when I do win, was there ever any doubt that I wouldn't.

I'd be the first boxer from Tyneside to do this so let's get in there, win that belt, and I can keep it forever, and that is what I did, I got in there and won – although I'm glad I didn't have to pay for fixing the ring, I'd pass on to Ronnie and Gary every day….

Not only did I become the first Tyneside boxer to achieve that feat of winning the British title outright (well done to Lewis Ritson in equally that feat in 2018), but I also became the first fighter to win titles and in order of Prizefighter (Northern) Area, English and British, it's no mean feat that mind.

The one thing that I really liked about winning that belt outright, as did my mother as well actually, was that I got to keep it and it's now something for my little man, Joseph-Lewis, to have when he's older, something we can be proud of.

What people may not know, or realise, is that, when you first win the British title, then defend it over and over again, you never have it for that long, the Boxing Board of Control kept taking it back.

Also, another brilliant thing about going for the British outright against Dawson, and although I wasn't a lucky mascot, I got to show it off on the hallowed turf at St James' Park, the home of Newcastle United (against Everton, the Toffees winning 3-0 that night).

I'm not an Arsenal fan, like that Prizefighter interview stated back in 2010 – moral there is, don't say things that aren't true as you don't know where they might end up. I told whoever interviewed me that Arsenal was my favourite team, and it was published – oops!

It was an amazing feeling being able to do something like that though as chances of that stature don't come along to often but I'm a champion and it's occasions like that which spurred me on.

Although nothing major materialised after I'd beaten Dawson, boxing becoming somewhat stagnated - I'd have loved to have mixed it with fighters of the calibre of Nathan Cleverly or maybe Ola Afolabi, or as you'll see later on, a few other big names, but boxing is a funny game and only the Simmons fight really stirred me.

We, Dawson and I, both had similar records going into that March showdown at the Arena.

I'd won 14 with three stoppages from my sixteen contests and he'd won 12 of his fourteen with five stoppages to his name but I knew that, if I stuck to the game plan and put in a performance I was capable of doing, doing what Ronnie and Gary in my corner had told me to, then I'd achieve the dream, we did exactly that.

It has been a really good career though, both in the amateurs and in the paid ranks during what, a near twenty year boxing career which begun back in the mid-nineties and went through until shortly after I lost, unfortunately, to Tommy McCarthy, in May 2016.

I've been through battles in and out of the ring.

I've won titles, both as an amateur and a professional.

I've represented my country.

I've married the love of my life in Kate and have the craziest, most wonderful son in Joseph-Lewis as well as two other children prior to Kate in (ADD NAMES)

I now have my own business as well.

And I can eat kebabs and any other takeaways which takes my fancy whenever I want.

I've made many friends, some of whom are as close as my family are and I've got several titles to my name.

This, with a little boxing history thrown into the mix as well, is my story. I am Jon-Lewis Dickinson and I'm…

Cruising to Glory

TWO

The Early Years

PEOPLE TEND TO FORGET THAT, before I was a professional boxer, I was a relatively successful amateur as well, although that in itself is a long time ago.

I'd not long since started at secondary school, I was about 10-11-years-old I think, and my grandad, Jack, put me straight into the local gym, it was from that point on that I would have a life of boxing, some twenty years in that ring – no wonder I look like I do, a right handsome b£&%*@d

Hass Hass...

I recall winning my first eight fights in the amateur game, better than my start as a pro at least, whilst at Chester Moor, but I'd never thought of turning pro for maybe five years or so if I'm honest.

Even before I started boxing I always wanted some Prince Naz (Naseem Hamed) shorts, you know the ones, all leopard print, pretty cool and snazzy they were.

Naz was a great fighter and I loved his style, I loved sitting and watching old fights and documentaries, I loved him and Roy Jones Jnr.

When I was about 15, maybe 16, I started thinking about the pros and realised that winning something called the Lord Lonsdale belt was the biggest thing, a dream for any British fighter to achieve, and it took me seventeen years to get to that point from when I first started out.

In those early yearly though, even before I started boxing, life was pretty good, school withstanding, and we never wanted for anything at all if I'm honest.

My mam will tell you that I was always the good child, honestly, well I'd like to that to be case anyway.

I WAS BORN IN EDMONDSLEY, a little village on the outskirts of County Durham to Jon and Jacqueline (Jacquie) Dickinson in the house that is literally right next door to the one in which my parents live now.

I wasn't their first child, and thankfully I wasn't the last either in our family. My older brother, Mark, he came first on January 31 1979, then it was our Leanne on November 23 1981; mum and dad then took a bit of a break in the baby stakes before I popped onto the scene on Saturday 3 May 1986, coming out a lovely, Taurean bull, then came our Travis close to seven years after my little sister - I think she'd have killed him if they shared the same birthday but our Travis' is four days earlier, arriving on November 19 1988.

And that was us, one big, happy family and we had fun growing up, although I eventually learned to hate school – didn't we all at some point in our childhood.

There's a few things that haven't changed for me since childhood, my likening for food, money, a familial love of boxing, Ireland, and horses.

Yes, horses.

I guess that's why I was drawn to Kate when I was older, no not because of her long drawn face you cheeky buggers, but her love for that fair breed of animal as well, among other things obviously.

You see, when I was younger, I used to own and race a pony, harnessed, called 'The Tarmac Cub,' it was a cracking animal and we won a good few races together.

I've always loved food though, even growing up, and mum is a fantastic cook – I guess she had to learn fast to look after all our food prep in later years.

Our Travis though, he used to fall for the same old joke every time we had our meals and he had something on his plate that I fancied to eat myself – you all know the one.

Whilst our kid was munching away I used to say to him "what's that over there" and nick his food from his plate when he turned away to look, it got him every time as well.

There was this one time, and I guess the best stories always revolve around food and drink with me, that our mum had ordered a takeaway and our kid didn't like it, he wanted a kebab instead.

I don't blame him on that score mind, nowt beats a good kebab...

Anyway, he didn't like not getting his own way so decided that he was going to run away from home instead. I told mum to wait until he got to the end of the street and I'd go out and fetch him back, which I did, whilst wearing five hats and carrying with me my trusty catapult.

I still can't think why I out the five hats on, maybe it was cold out, or our Travis needed one for his head, but the catapult was to catch myself a few rabbits and cook them as well.

We always fought as well, used to lock ourselves away in the barns where the horses were kept and scrap, and I mean scrap as well.

We used to beast each other until the other couldn't stand, but that was us, it really was.

I did the important thing though and caught up with Travis, bringing him home with his tail between his legs, the numpty, as I'd promised mum I'd do.

As for money, who doesn't like a bit of hard-earned cash?

I have loved money from a very early age, and that was for me, nobody else.

I recall my mum used to keep saying, when I wanted something, that I should use my money to get this and that to which I'd sharp fire back, "why should I, I'm not spending any of my money."

I like the finer things in life as well, I always have done, I just don't like to pay for them myself.

As for going to school, I never liked that place.

I guess the juniors was alright, but the seniors, I just didn't like it, and nothing endeared itself to me in regards of education.

I never got away with doing schoolwork and would rather have been outside either with the horses we had, or playing football, or doing something, anything, but sitting in a classroom.

I eventually ended up doing a bricklaying course, which I really enjoyed, but then, when I did the joinery course afterwards, I ended up doing those exams anyway which I would have done had I stayed at school.

I felt cheated!

We had a few sporting interests, particularly Travis and I, although our Mark used to box a little as well before us two.

My sporting passions were horses, football and boxing and Travis used to ride his bike a lot, and throw things, the javelin mainly.

Our parents used to go and watch a local boxer called John 'Dava' Davison as our Aunt Betty, who used to own a jewellers shop in Newcastle, sponsored him (Davison fought between 1989 and 1992, winning the British and WBC International featherweight titles, he retired with a record of 15-5; 9); and there was a bloke called Michael 'Mick' Mason from Sunderland, also in the nineties (his record was 11-2-2; 1).

Before I took to boxing myself though my dad took me to karate classes and believe me, I wasn't no Karate Kid that's for sure.

I was like five years old and they took me to some place over Grange Villa. I quickly put paid to that daft idea though, happily exclaiming after a session that "I wasn't going back there, they can break your arms."

So I chose boxing and getting my nose broke instead – I did tell you I was a mad bugger.

Boxing though would very soon become, and consume, my life and that's mainly down to my grandad, good ol' Jack Dickinson, that and because there was, quite literally, nothing to do in old Edmondsley other than hang around the street corners and in bus shelters, and our parents weren't going to let us do that.

So, grandad, who himself used to go to Craghead in his younger days with a couple of lads called Terry and Leo, who I believe worked for the National Coal Board and, although grandad never boxed himself, he loved going and taking us along with him.

I'm sure it was some sort of punishment that we enjoyed doing, no, can we not use that one as an excuse?

Our Travis didn't like going initially and jacked it in early to throw some stick about and run around in circles like a headless chicken, javelin and athletics.

We were still kids though, I was what, ten or eleven years old when we were taken to Chester Moor and my first contest, at the Marriott Hotel, was against some lad called K. Dodd yeah, even we thought I was fighting Ken Dodd!

There's still that thought, even looking back now, that I did the right thing with both myself and Travis going down to Chester Moor first and they had some decent trainers there, and a pretty decent set-up.

I remember that, when we first started looking at moving over to Birtley ABC a few years later that there was something of a waiting list but we were told not to worry, we'd get a spot there.

It was the best fighting gym in the region even then as well and the McLean's were the main boxing kids, Andy McLean was something rather special.

Down at Chester Moor it was more of a one-man band, we were guided by a bloke called Alan Alderson, who was a stalwart at the gym and a really good bloke, whereas at Birtley there was a few people doing the business including Graeme Rutherford and some bloke called Ronnie Rowe.

I did alright in the juniors as well, probably better than the seniors really and won the Junior ABA's in both 2003 and 2004, an NABC title in 2003, alongside represented my country and winning a Four Nations Gold medal, also in 2003, for added measure.

In 2001 I fought a lad called Tony Hill from Southampton, he was coached by Stuey Gill, in the schoolboy championships – it was a very defining fight for me to be honest.

Facing Tony changed me and made me realise, during that early fight, that I could do something in boxing.

It was at the Barnsley Metrodome if I recall correctly, and he was all over me in the first round and was very confident that he was going to knock me out but I caught him at the end of the first and put him down but the bell saved him.

In the second I pushed him all over and thought I'd done enough to nick it at the end but ultimately he did. After that fight we both went on to win the Junior ABA's, the Four Nations, and roomed together with the England squad on occasion as well.

It was in 2003 that I beat a lad called James DeGale in the final (DeGale would go on to be a successful amateur and professional boxer winning gold at the 2008 Beijing Olympics as well as earning bronze at the 2006 Commonwealth Games and silver at successive European Championships before winning a plethora of middleweight and super middleweight titles).

That year I also won the NABC title against Jamie Weston, and a Four Nations gold medal beating the Irishman Daniel Daley.

In 2004 I achieved a second successive Junior ABA title whilst never having a full fight, stopping S. Keogh from Liverpool's Gemini club in the final.

The seniors though, well that was a bit hit and miss – just ask that man Bellew!

JACQUIE DICKINSON (JON-LEWIS' mother)

He was a funny kid was our Jon-Lewis, and always trying to imitate people.

I'm pleased that all four of our kids got on though, most of the time, although if you ask me then Jon-Lewis was always going to kill our Travis.

My boys did have an early interest in boxing before they started at Chester Moor, in fact there used to be photos of Jon-Lewis and Travis as kids, in hooded dressing gowns and boxing gloves, posing in our front yard.

I went to and, just about, watched almost every bout as well, only missing a couple, once because of work and another, well because I was in Ireland and we have Irish blood in us.

They never wanted an easy ride though, they always wanted to fight the toughest, the best that the sport has to offer.

I used to do all their meals, for both Jon-Lewis and Travis, breakfast, dinner and tea, and I loved it when they were training, it was lovely seeing them so focussed – we've been everywhere in the UK, to the USA, Germany, Ireland, and even to Azerbaijan with these boys.

LEANNE DICKINSON (JON-LEWIS' sister)

To be honest I was always the bad influence when we were younger, sneaking out of the house with me but we did clash, a lot.

When we were younger Jon-Lewis and I clashed badly. He always though he was the boss of me because he was the boy and I knew I was the boss because I was older.

He used to always beat the life out of me, mainly because he was a stubborn bugger, and he'd always go off and do something, get something, just to spite me because I couldn't do it.

I went to most of his amateur fights, even calling in sick at work to go and watch both him and Travis fight –work knew I was doing it as well to be honest and I loved it. They were pretty good times as well, especially going to Dungarven in Ireland – just don't ask me about those bloody bibles.

One thing that he was really good at though, and I mean side-splittingly, tears in your eyes, stomach achingly funny, was his impersonating.

He always had this amazing sense of humour and would often cheer gran up when she was down, especially doing his Jim Carey (The Mask) impersonation whilst attempting to play the piano – that I'm afraid, he can't do.

11

THREE

THE ABA's & BELLEW

WE HAD some pretty good times in the amateur ranks, from joining Chester Moor, then moving on to Birtley, first with Graeme Rutherford then under Ronnie Rowe, who I would spend the majority of my amateur, and professional career with.

I would represent my country on a number of occasions, winning a Four Nations Gold medal as well as a few other, amateur titles. However, the two, standout moments from my time then would arrive in the Senior ABA's.

In 2005 I would reach the heavyweight (91kg) finals before losing, well actually I was stopped, by a certain Tony Bellew; and then, two years later, in 2007, I won the cruiserweight (86kg) version against Mark Redhead.

Bellew's win over me, he was with Rotunda ABC at the time, it was his second success of three-in-a-row (David Dolan of Sunderland ABC won the heavyweight version in 2000, 2001 and 2002; Warren Baister, also of Sunderland, won in 2008 and 2014), whilst in 2007, in what was only the sixth at that weight and the first in five years, I defeated Redhead (James Dolan of Plains Farm ABC claimed a hat-trick in 2000, 2001 and 2002).

Although I won the ABA's in 2007, the run to the 2005 final, and then losing Bellew, which was more down to my own doing than anything he threw at me, is the more vivid of the two memories, the one that stands out the most.

You have to realise that, back then, I hated Bellew with a passion, and that played into why he defeated me in the final.

He got himself into my head, my mind, so I actually beat myself – that would never happen again.

I was up on points in that final, everyone could see that and I was even the better boxer, I knew I could have out boxed him but he did his job rather well.

When I first saw him he was mouthing stuff towards me and I'd already done quite a bit in the competition to get that far as it was.

I was originally an 81 kilos boxer and had to go up ten to 91 in order to compete as there was no weight classes in between in which I could enter into, but I wasn't going to miss out on such an opportunity.

I remember defeating a lad called China Clarke en route to the final, I stopped him in the second round – he's a great lad and we sparred quite a lot in the pro game as well (China had a 14-1-1; 1 pro career between 2009 and 2013 winning the English title against Wadi Camacho in his final year), then I beat Tom Dallas who was also a good bloke, we knew each other rather well due to us training together in the England squad (Dallas had a 17-10; 12 fight record between 2008 and 2017, challenging for the Southern Area and WBO NABA heavyweight straps) and Mike O'Connell, rather convincingly, on points in the semi-finals.

I watched as Bellew launched his semi-final opponent, literally, all over the ring and, after he'd won, he came out of the ring and straight over to me, he motioned towards me, mouthing things at me, and I went away that day, hating him.

People were warning me, between the semi and the final, that he was a big puncher, but I wanted to go in there on finals day and kill him, smash him up, I hated him that much.

Therefore, I spent the next two weeks being unable to sleep and, on the day of the final, we had a few gripes, I just wanted to jump him right there and then.

When that first bell went, at the start of the heavyweight final, I just went straight for him, all guns blazing; I didn't want to just beat him, but he did me and more by getting into my mind than anything else and he just bided his time – he'd really done a good number on me.

In his post-fight interview he admitted that's what he'd done and why he'd done it, that basically I had lost the fight because he'd managed to get into my head. I lost that 2005 final myself and I learnt a whole lot more because of that fact.

Now though, Bellew is actually a really nice bloke and we've spoken to each other on a number of occasions, he going on to have a rather decent career of his own.

After I'd lost to Bellew I remember travelling over to Dungarven, Ireland, with the amateurs and fought a lad called Alan Reynolds, he was the Irish champion seven times back then and was one of two brothers (Stephen was also very distinguished), Alan even won five-in-a-row.

I went over there and beat him on points.

However, the rematch at The Fed, in Dunstonn, he beat me on a spilt point's decision, and broke my bloody nose which meant I couldn't enter the 2006 ABA's, which was a shame really.

RONNIE ROWE – (long-time coach, mentor, friend, and manager; Birtley ABC & Fighting Chance Promotions)

When Jon-Lewis came to me at Birtley I was looking after the senior boxers, and Graeme Rutherford the juniors and it wasn't until he was around 17 he moved into my senior set-up.

He went into the ABA's when he was 18 I believe and we didn't really want him to due to his lack of experience at the senior level but he managed to stop everyone on his way to facing Bellew in the final.

The final, against Bellew, was such a shame really, the way things happened, as he was doing so well in the first two rounds but he came back two years later to win at a lighter weight.

We knew, even then, in him that he wanted to turn professional.

• • •

KELLIE MALONEY — (formerly Frank Maloney, boxing promoter and manager of both Dickinson brothers)

I knew Jon-Lewis even from his amateur days, when he was fighting in the ABA's.

I already knew that he was good fighter and I was looking to expand in the north-east and already had Tony Jeffries on my books.

Jon-Lewis had that great fight with Tony Bellew in the 2005 ABA finals and people told me that I shouldn't bother, he had no bottle, but I totally disagreed with that point.

As FOR THE rest of my time in the amateurs, winning the 2007 cruiser-weight (86kg), a victory which also saw me win the Tyneside Senior Boxer of the Year Award (Birtley also claimed the Champions Cup that year via the Tyneside Ex-Boxers Association) so it was actually a pretty good year for me.

They'd just re-introduced the cruiserweight limit the year I got my hands on the gold which was good news for me.

The heavier weights were alright, I wouldn't have got to the final if it wasn't, but I was better at the lighter weights and so it proved that year when I reached the final again, this time winning at the famous York Hall.

I beat a lad called D. Ward from Belgrave before opposing Tom Watson from the Golden Ring gym at Liverpool's Olympia. I'm sure Watson did some training up here at Birtley and fought that bloke Katie Price was with, Alex, in MMA as well.

Facing Mark Redhead in the ABA final was an interesting one as he used to be always there or thereabouts when it came to the amateur finals weekends and was a good age, very experienced, when I boxed him.

I'll tell you one thing though, I sued to be a rather aggressive boxer until I faced Bellew, that fight with him changed my style and manner of how I approached fights, and fighters.

• • •

ONE OF THE people early in the Dickinson story, behind-the –scenes, was Lewis Pendleton.

Whilst working for Gateshead Council Lewis would come to know Ronnie Rowe and, in turn, others at Birtley ABC whilst being 'dragged' into becoming an integral part of the Dickinson mantra. Later down the line he would, alongside Ronnie Rowe, create Fighting Chance Promotions.

Speaking of those early years Lewis said: "I met Ronnie when I was working for Gateshead Council as their Sport Development Officer when I was tasked with looking after boxing in Gateshead and to create a boxing development group within the area.

"I swore back then that I would never work for the club (Birtley) bought Ronnie made me buy into it, him and Paul Bentley who was one of the trustees at the time.

"I remember Travis going out to Azerbaijan and winning the Presidents Cup, Craig (Dixon) and Gary (Barr) were doing really well also, and I was going to amateur shows all the time. Little did I know that I would be working with them for the next fifteen years!

"I'd watched the lads but never really had any direct involvement with them although I've always thought of myself as a fan prior to Jon-Lewis leaving and going with Glenn McCrory and Micky Duncan. "

FOUR

Turning Professional

AT SOME POINT, in early 2008, I made the decision to leave the amateur ranks and become a professional, get paid for being punched in the face…

It could have been seen as being a daft decision at the time, my family kind of felt that way if I'm honest, plus I had to leave my mentor and coach, Ronnie Rowe, in order to turn professional.

The daft old bugger didn't have a pro manager's licence back then so myself, and brother Travis, ended up turning over under the guidance of some bloke called Frank Maloney; he's now Kellie and I'll tell you more on that later.

Anyway, here I was turning professional, and I wasn't even going to be making my debut at home, they actually made me travel to some place called the Robin Park Centre in Wigan and face some bloke called Paul Bonson – he'd made his debut some twelve years before me so was something of an old-timer and had won twenty fights, including the Southern Area heavyweight strap.

Although he'd lost more than he'd won I must have been crazy, we must have been, to go and take a fight like that, it was my debut and anything could happen.

I mean come on, this bloke Bonson had fought a few decent names as well before he faced me – Enzo Maccarinelli, Carl Froch, Neil Dawson (more on him as well), Ovill McKenzie (and him), Mike Stafford (yeah, him as well) and, a couple of weeks after I'd beaten him, another of my future opponents, Matty Askin, would make his debut as well against Bonson – that bloke may have lost over a hundred times but only three managed to stop him, one of those wasn't me.

Boxing can be crazy like that, it really can.

Anyway, that man Maloney promoted the show down Wigan, it was the night Lee Haskins won the British super flyweight title against Andy Bell. Scott Quigg was on the undercard as well, and I won on points, the referee, Steve Gray, awarding me a 40-36 win - cheers for that one mate!

When I signed with Maloney we all knew that I'd be fighting on the road, there was more opportunities that way back then and, after I'd outpointed Bonson in Wigan I found myself at the Fenton Manor Sports Complex in Stoke against a lad from Donny called John Anthony.

At that time Anthony was holding a 6-9 (4) losing record but was still pretty dangerous and, although he won two more over the next few years, it was a good test for me.

The fight with Anthony was on the undercard of a British & Commonwealth flyweight scrap between Chris Edwards and Wayne Bloy, as well as fighters like Paul Edwards, Larry Olubamiwo, Scott Lawton, and Ashley Sexton on the undercard, I myself did enough to claim a second points win with the referee, Robert Chalmers, reeling off another 40-36 score in my favour.

After those two wins on the road Maloney had wrapped up the signature of Tony Jeffries (2008 Beijing Olympics bronze medallist) who is the son of Wearside promoter/manager, Phil Jeffries.

It was around then that Jaffa (Phil Jeffries) began putting shows on in the north-east giving us more of a platform, although his son Tony unfortunately had to wrap his career up early due to bad hands.

(Phil Jeffries put two shows on in 2008 and one in 2010 at the Rainton Meadows Arena before the first Summer Rumble in July 2011).

The 2009 Maloney promotion at the Crowtree Leisure Centre was a really good fight card with some cracking local talent on show.

I fought Nick Okoth that night, for the first time, over four rounds, and there was outings for people like Paul Holborn, Danny Hughes, Tony Jeffries, and our Travis as well, all the local lads picking up solid victories although mine was narrower than most people, including myself, actually thought but Graeme Williams felt otherwise and gave it 39-38 in my favour (he also refereed the fights for both Hughes and our Travis that night) whilst the main events would see successes for Jamie Moore and Rendall Munroe.

Two months later and myself, and our kid, were back out again, this time at the Seaburn Centre; big David Ferguson fought that night, as did young Jeffries, Trevor Crewe ad Chris Mullen.

My opponent was the Birmingham-based journeyman, Hastings Rasani (he's from Zimbabwe initially) who also had near a hundred fights in his career; he'd topped sixty when he faced me.

He'd also come from pretty good stock as well having challenged for, and won, titles earlier in his career, but his last win prior to facing myself was some three years earlier.

I wasn't going to let my record drop though that's for sure and, as with my previous fight, referee Williams was the man in charge and he gave me my fourth pro win, this one with a slightly better winning margin my winning 40-37.

That year, 2009, was going to be a busy one for me and, having taken my record to 4-0 it was a lad called Martyn Grainger, who would be the fighter to lead me into the Prizefighter tournament with an unblemished record.

At that particular time Grainger had won three of his first four outings so we were quite evenly matched I guess.

Again our kid was on the same fight card as me, he was taking care of a debutant called Steffan Hughes; Hartlepool's Michael Hunter lost a British title scrap to Jason Booth, and there were performances from talents like George Groves and David Price, both of whom went on to have pretty decent careers themselves.

Again Mr Williams was charged with my contest and would give me a second 40-37 score, I think he liked me a little bit bless him.

I'd now had a decent start to my career in the paid ranks, I'd won my first five contests as a professional boxer, and Duncan, whilst at Howdon, had guided me (along with the likes of Dougie Curran and Mark Clauzel who were in the same gym at the time) rather well to be honest but, inside me, I wasn't fully happy, I wasn't a hundred percent mentally in the game – and before you all say anything, I know I've not been a hundred percent right in the head.

Hass! Hass!

RONNIE ROWE SAID of Jon-Lewis turning professional: "Back then, when Jon-Lewis turned professional in 2008, amateur coaches weren't allowed to look after or train professional boxers, the boxing board always being a body to constantly change things though.

"It was in those early days that Jon-Lewis went to Glenn McCrory's gym and was trained by Micky Duncan, however, for Jon-Lewis, things weren't quite working out for him there and, although he'd won his first five fights, the last against Martyn Grainger in Sunderland, he felt things needed changing.

"That's when he came back to me at Birtley, we sat down and had a good chat about things; I remember him thinking at that time that he wanted to pack it all in but asked if I'd consider giving things a go (he was managed by Frank Maloney in those early days).

"We spoke on a provisional basis and things were really good, it was just like old times when we were in the amateurs and that's when we got the call to go try the Prizefighter, and everything changed."

KELLIE MALONEY, who guided the early stages of Jon-Lewis' career, added: "Jon-Lewis came to me from day one and was actually recommended to me.

I met with his mother and father, who are very lovely people, a really nice couple however boxing, in all honesty, it had died a death in the north-east after McCrory, Hardy etc, but I was looking for new areas to expand myself into and, in finding Jon-Lewis, I believed I could build the regions' fan-base around him.

I had to hit it off with fighters though, fighters that I represented, to have a bonding with them, otherwise there's no real point.

I felt that I hit it off with Jon-Lewis though, and his family, from the start, and I was happy to sign him up as he was not only a good fighter but had a lot of skill.

With Ronnie as well, we got on really well and we both left each other to get on with our respective jobs. He'd call me to ask advise but never queried who I put Jon-Lewis (or Travis) in the ring with, that was good. I liked that respect in which they showed me, that they trusted my judgement.

I set about building Jon-Lewis' career the way it should have been built, like a stepping stone career.

I always had a lot of faith in Jon-Lewis as well and really believed that he'd become a champion, I just didn't know as to what level.

I knew that it would be at least to British level, which would be in his grasp, but I also was aware that there was a dark side to the Dickinson's as well, but our relationship grew and Jon-Lewis would always be ready to fight and never pulled out.

IT WAS NOW COMING towards the end of 2009 for me and, as was usually the case during my career, amateur or professional, I needed a new challenge, something new, something different in order to get me going again.

Mind you, an added bonus come the New Year was the addition of a pretty decent woman to my life. I suppose I have to give a few mentions to Kate Williams (now Dickinson) who I managed to not only get to agree to be my girl but she also got lucky and became my beloved wife as well as the mother of our son over the next ten years, and more.

I guess you'd say she's something of a good egg, I suppose she is really.

Spilling the beans on their getting together and the early part of their love for each other Kate Dickinson said of her husband: "There's always been a debate about how we got together so I'll set the record straight here and now shall I?

"I added him on Facebook back in 2010, I mean everybody added everybody else back then and he tried to talk to me, chat me up, straight away.

21

"And yes, I ignored him!

"Then he put some funny post on about a snowman which I commented on and that's when we started messaging each other.

"It didn't take him long to ask me for my number and he's harassed me pretty much every day since really.

"I remember that all my friends and family were calling him Lewis all the time because when I did add him on Facebook he was in his boxing gear and his shorts had that on them, that's what I thought his name was and I saved him in my phone as that.

"I'm also taking credit for his nickname change to J-Lo as I changed his Facebook name to that and it well, kind of stuck.

"I was never really into boxing though, when we got together – do you all see what he's done to me?

"Not long after we got together though he went into that Prizefighter tournament and he rings me up telling me about it, and that he's going to be on the television and all that.

"Here's me though, completely oblivious, paying no attention, not bothered at all.

"But, I invite all my friends round to watch it on the night and it's a good job he won or I'd have dumped him straight away.

"How embarrassing would his losing have been for me in front of my friends and family?

"He's still rather dramatic though, even now, like he was back then; I always tell him he's having a mariah and boy does he love a bit of gossip, getting to know all the craic."

SHE'S one in a million though and I'm glad she stuck with me; I think I'm glad I also went and won Prizefighter as well, lord knows what would have happened otherwise.

But that was it, five fights done, five wins on the record, and I'd gone and got myself a smart girl – happy days.

Now though it was time to go to work, to do the business.

It was time to go and pocket that 32k prize money and start creating history.

FIVE

Prizefighter Champion

ALL I HAD to do on that night back in 2010 was to box what was put in front of me, it's all any boxer can do, granted I had to face three opponents in one night but it was worth it, not only for the prize money, but also for the prestige of being called 'Prizefighter Champion.'

I'd won all five my previous contests, against Paul Bonson, John Anthony, Nick Okoth, Hastings Rasani, and Martyn Grainger, so I was rather confident and yes, I wanted the glory and was looking forward to the night immensely.

The one thing that I wasn't willing to do was go in there and lose my unbeaten record, I wanted to come out of it 8-0 and with that trophy in hand, which I did.

Looking back now I still believe I was made for a tournament like that, and no fighter wants losses on their record either so I guess it was also a risk for me going into it unbeaten.

Fighters from the north-east have entered Prizefighter both before, and after me – David Ferguson, David Dolan, Chris Burton, Glenn Foot, and our Travis, the latter two having won their respective competitions but for me it was all about that night in April 2010.

Walking out to the ring, in the famous York Hall, and winning a tournament like that, the way in which I did, was exhilarating to say the least.

There were some good names in the competition that night, including the former WBO heavyweight champion, Herbie Hide, but I was expecting nothing less than victory.

I'd not long since got the girl, and now I wanted the trophy to add some shine.

Having someone of the calibre of Herbie Hide (nicknamed the Dancing Destroyer, Hide fought between 1989 and 2010, retiring with a record of 49-4; 43, and won British, WBC International and WBO World heavyweight titles and the WBC International cruiserweight strap) in the same competition as me was actually a great feeling prior to the competition.

We knew beforehand that a big name was going to be involved and that gave me something in which to focus on, a challenge, and a target if I was to succeed.

I wasn't a twelve round fighter at the time I went into the tournament, crikey I wasn't even at championship level, the furthest I'd gone prior to that night was four, and my last two bouts hadn't even got past three..

However, a tournament like this was set at three fights over three rounds apiece, if I was to go all the way so, in essence, that made this a sprint, not a marathon.

The likes of Herbie Hide, former Commonwealth champion Darren Corbett, former British heavyweight champion Mark Krence, they'd all done longer rounds and had benefitted from it. To me though, they'd had their careers, their time in the spotlight so to speak.

It was still going to be tough though and the draw pitted me against Leon Williams, who had a 4-1(2) record going into the night.

The remainder of the draw for the cruiserweight Prizefighter would see Mark Krence oppose Zahid Kahut, John Anthony against Darren Corbett, and Wayne Brooks drew Herbie Hide.

It was to be a night of many twists and turns for all of us, that's for sure.

Herbie was, rightly so, the pre-tournament favourite, after all, that experience and success he'd ascertained spoke volumes.

I mean even before the Prizefighter he'd won 48 of 52 contests and stopped 43 of them, his four losses had also come by way of a stoppage as well.

It really would have been my facing him but he bottled it, knowing that he would be facing a young upstart like me in the final.

Seriously though, look at what he had done in his career, he didn't have to go and fight that night, did he?

Of his four losses, one was against Riddick Bowe and another against Vitali Klitschko, that's some level to be at and just imagine if the fifth loss read Jon-Lewis Dickinson.

Hass! Hass!

The titles he'd won, he'd done most of them whilst I was still at school as well, jeez.

When I was eight he was heavyweight champion of the world, stopping Michael Bentt is seven for the WBO in London back in March '94, he won it again three years later, and I'm still at school.

I bet you're all thinking that the organisers had put an old man in this tournament now aren't you?

Hide was still going when I made my pro debut in 2008, he'd won and defended the WBC International strap around 2007 and 2008 so to me, facing Hide, I guess even at that age, would have been a good name, a massive scalp, to have on my record.

It wasn't to be though – he didn't lose mind, he defeated his opponent, Wayne Brooks, via unanimous decision over three whilst I defeated Williams on a split in my opening bout.

The other two quarter-final contests would see victories for Mark Krence and Darren Corbett.

Hide had defeated Brooks but, due to an 'injury' he'd sustained from a clash of heads, needed medical advice and withdrew from the competition and it was down to a coin toss to see which of the reserve fighters would step into the fray.

Former opponent Nick Okoth was afforded that honour, I'd faced him a year before when winning my third professional contest, in fact

I'd also beaten another Prizefighter combatant, John Anthony as well, in my second outing but, with Hide resigned to the injured list, and my defeating Williams, I'd become more confident of success.

Having watched Hide's fight with Brooks I still say I'd have beaten him anyway.

My facing Williams was a close fight but I can't see how the judges gave the scores the way in which they did though. I know that I won the first two round comfortably and, even though the third was pretty close, in my eyes I'd gone out there and won that fight by a bigger margin – if I was to have faced Williams again I knew I'd have dominated him.

In the semis I breezed past Mark Krence, he retired on his stool at the end of the first round and Okoth had beaten Darren Corbett in the other via unanimous decision and that set up myself versus Okoth for the second time as professionals, this time in the Prizefighter final.

Even though just short of a year had passed since Okoth on points at the Crowtree Leisure Centre, just up the road in Sunderland (now that was some fight card), I went into that final and showed him how much I'd improved, that not only my fitness but everything else was now at a completely different level.

I'd gone back to Birtley prior to entering this and was working with Ronnie, my old amateur coach, again. I was in fantastic condition so to be able to show how far I'd actually come was a great feeling, not only for me but for my team as well.

It wasn't hard fighting Okoth the second time around either. Far from it, and I think I controlled the fight quite easily, everything I had in me was just too good for him on the night.

It showed because I went and stopped him in the third round, giving me that lush cup, and the thirty-two grand that was on offer didn't I.

Hass! Hass!

The Hide situation still irks with me though, that was a bit of a bummer really, a sickener, not only for me as a fighter but also for fight fans everywhere.

He pulled out in order to keep his ranking and never boxed again. Come on, what's all that about?

Honestly, everybody that was there that night, and I mean everybody, will tell you the same thing – Herbie Hide feared getting beat off Jon-Lewis Dickinson, he had nowhere to Hide. I think we had a tee-shirt made up for that specific thing as well.

After all, Hide waited until I'd beaten Krence in the semis, and I'd retired him at the end of the first, and then, when I was being interviewed after that fight, that was when it was announced he'd withdrawn, right then, at that moment.

I'd entered the competition with zero intentions of being beaten though and I knew that he, Hide, was going to be competing, we all did.

Don't get me wrong here, he wasn't at his best, his peak, it wasn't the Herbie Hide that had been world champion over twelve rounds, but it was still Herbie Hide and he was the one that getting nervous.

I definitely believe that I'd have beaten Hide that night and he pulled out die to that fact, and he knows that as well.

I guess we'll never know what would have happened.

Winning the Prizefighter is certainly up there with being the best night of my life, as a professional boxer that is – winning this, the British title, and defeating Simbo, they were great times.

I really enjoyed a night like this from start to finish and it wasn't just about the boxing either, the atmosphere, the build-up, was amazing.

It all came together because we'd put all the graft in beforehand and I don't think I've ever felt as fit as I did that night either.

The challenge that was placed in front of me drove me on and winning it just made things a whole lot easier for me, gave me better options afterwards as well, both personally and professionally.

I spoke with my promoter, Frank Maloney, straight after the tournament and we both understood what was needed next for me, I needed to go out and get rounds under my belt,

Although that somehow became something of a struggle in my next two outings, for one reason or another so getting the rounds eventually took a little doing, but we did it.

For me though, the next challenge after those successive losses to Tyrone Wright and Richard Turba would be my heading into enemy territory and challenging the home favourite, David Dolan, for the Northern Area cruiserweight title.

It wouldn't be the first time Dolan and I met either.

On that Prizefighter success mentor Ronnie Rowe said: "It was an exhilarating performance and I was absolutely ecstatic with the outcome.

"It was a new experience for me despite everything I had done at amateur level.

"We sat down and looked at the different fighters that Jon-Lewis was in line to face on the night and the tactics which we put together were spot on.

"To me, he's always been a big talent and he got his reward in the Prizefighter; he was very inexperienced but had a fine future ahead of him."

A young Jon-Lewis
practicing his posing

Jon-Lewis
Dickinson aged
3 months
(approx)

Back: Mark &
Leanne
Front : Jon-Lewis
& Travis

Father and Sons

Jon Dickinson
with Jon-Lewis
& Travis

Jon-Lewis and Travis
atop a wonderfully
pleasing hippo!

Jon-Lewis and Travis
with Poppy, Sonny
and Tyson
(6 weeks)
Summer '92

Jon-Lewis chilling
in the playing fields

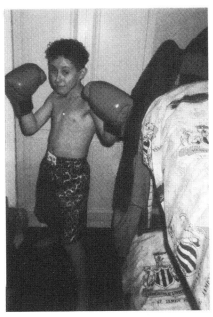

Sporting his Prince
Naz shorts!

An early start for
Jon-Lewis

'Once a poser!'

In those Prince Naz
shorts again!

Jon-Lewis, Leanne
and Travis

Jon-Lewis ready for
the seniors ABA's

L-R John Davison,
Travis Dickinson,
Leanne Dickinson
and Jon-Lewis
(holding an early set
of Dava's belts)

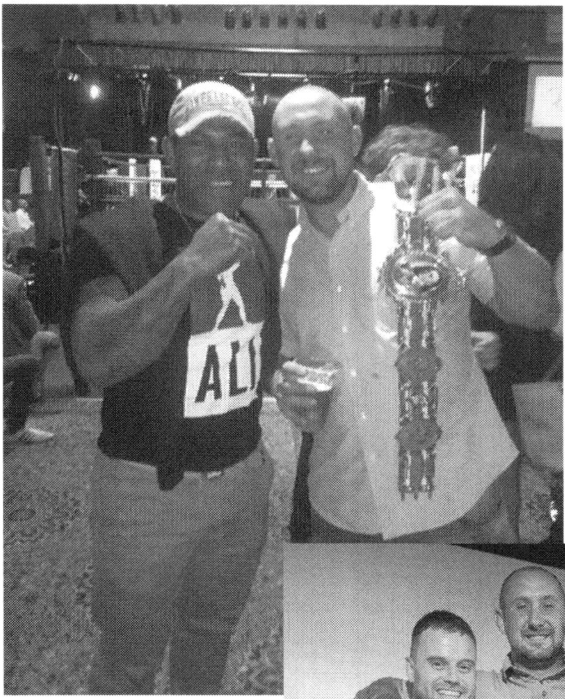
ALI

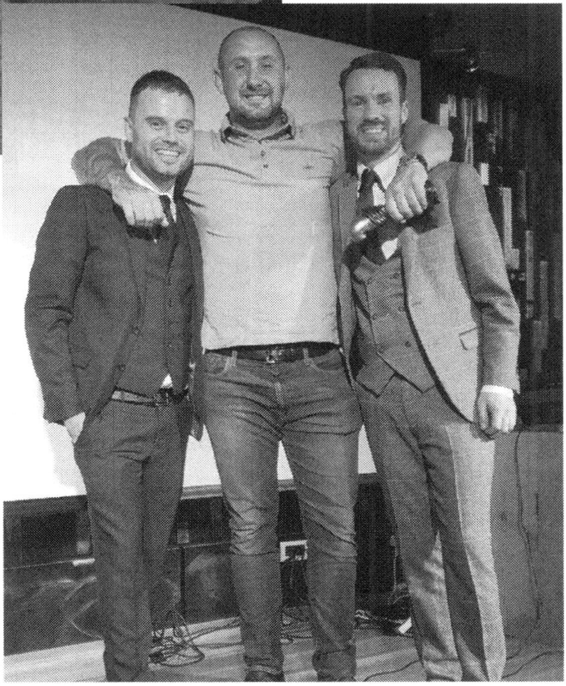

SIX

Area Champion

Wow, the Northern Area cruiserweight title, my first, official, professional boxing belt.

I was coming off the back of two defeats, two rather bad ones if I'm honest, against Tyrone Wright and Richard Turba, and that Prizefighter success the year before really did suddenly seem like a lifetime ago – it does even more now.

This was to be my eleventh outing as a professional, and I'd won eight of them whilst my opponent, local rival and hometown favourite, David Dolan, was a more established, experienced fighter.

He'd been there, where I wanted to be myself and envisioned being in the not-to-distant future; he'd challenged for the English, British and Commonwealth titles, was well respected in the fight game, but had come up short, twice, against Rob Norton.

He'd also been in the Prizefighter tournament, as a heavyweight, and I knew that, because of all that, he'd be my biggest challenge to date.

A ten round war meant just that, and I had to go and fight him again as well, ain't I just the nicest guy.

Anyway, it's July 2011 and Frank Maloney is co-promoter of the now-annual Summer Rumble at the Stadium of Light (don't worry, I won't swear, hass hass).

Frank, or Kellie as she is now, was very instrumental in my early fight career, this was also the case not only for our Travis, but also Tony Jeffries and Stuart Hall, both of who are great lads and fighters who've done a lot for the regions sport, and he also did a lot for the region at the same time.

So, having Frank, and Phil Jeffries, co-promote what is Jaffa's baby, was brilliant for all involved, especially myself and Davey who would headline.

Did I use the fight with Davey to eradicate those two losses? In a way I guess I did – a third defeat was not an option and would have meant a major rethink whilst victory, and the Area title, would open doors for me.

I also knew that the sparring I had in the build-up was good enough, both at Birtley, where I was based, and on the road with the likes of Turba, Mike Stafford, and big David Price, just for added fun really.

In all seriousness though, that sparring helped me no end and I've always been appreciative of anyone who's helped me over the years, and the assistance I got in all my title fights was second-to-none.

I knew what I wanted though and it wasn't just the area title, I wanted a crack at the British which, at that time, was held by Rob Norton.

He'd already beaten Dolan twice for that and the Commonwealth straps so, if I could get past Dolan then I knew where I'd be at and what I had to do to get there.

Coincidentally, after I'd beaten Dolan and won the Area title, Norton went and lost the British strap to, of all people, Leon Williams, whom I'd previously taken care of in the Prizefighter, then he went and lost it to Shane McPhilbin.

If you're not keeping up with this tale then I'm knackered that's for sure.

So, back to the Summer Rumble at a poor man's St. James' Park, and a fight which I was more than ready for.

Was it a tough ten rounds? Too rights it was and I think that, even looking back, I needed those rounds after what had happened in the previous two outings, even if it was a close result, referee Mark Curry giving me the result 97-94.

I'd never had as much bad luck as I'd had on the two fights previous either, I mean, come on, a swollen eye in the first and a broken jaw in the second didn't bode well.

Plus I'd been out of the sport for nearly nine months prior to opposing Dolan however I'd come back bigger and stronger and happier in myself so I suppose the injuries kind of worked in my favour.

That broken jaw, against Richard Turba, was the worst thing that could have happened to me but it did help in other ways.

Our kid had entered the Prizefighter at light heavyweight so I was roped into helping him for that. It blew away any cobwebs I may have had as Travis can be a right vicious bugger when he wants to be and, whether I should have done or not, we sparred quite a bit as well, which benefitted us both.

My facing Dolan I guess was destined to happen really, should really have happened earlier though, in the amateurs, but obviously didn't.

We'd come close to facing each other in my first year in the amateurs but he bottled it, nah, seriously, everyone in the region but myself had pulled out, including Davey, who was concentrating on international duties at the time.

I still think that even now I'd have like that fight we had at the Rumble to have been something bigger but, as he'd lost his fight when challenging for the English, it wasn't meant to be. I was however destined for bigger titles and bigger nights.

Having sparred Davey plenty enough prior to us being announced as opposing each other I was confident going into this contest and I knew that I would get that all-important win.

I had to, it was, in all honesty, a career-defining victory for me, and so it proved.

It was a really good fight as well that's for sure and of course I'm going to say I had the upper-hand and I guess my strength and staying power held up, more with the uppercuts I despatched. I was landing more in the closing stages and I most certainly used the momentum I'd built up against Davey to through future title contests.

Before this I'd never gone past four rounds.

My first five outings had all been points successes, the Prizefighter were all three rounders', mind you could say I was down for nine rounds that night but there was breaks between each fight as well, the two losses both were within three rounds.

Dolan meanwhile had two twelve round fights against Rob Norton and a handful of six round outings, before we clashed.

The fact he'd not long since lost to Terry Dunstan may have played on his mind a little but for me, I wanted that shot at Norton.

Maloney had said to me right before the Dolan fight that when I won this, Norton would be next, which gave me the added incentive I needed. Norton was the benchmark I saw myself aiming towards, he'd won the WBU, English, British and Commonwealth titles at one point or other during the previous decade.

For me, there was nothing else.

I wanted Rob Norton.

He had to go and lose to Leon Williams and the ballgame changed right then.

You have to remember though, I'd not been past four before facing Dolan so going in against Norton would have been an impressive challenge, not only for me, but any fighter faced with that scenario.

I'd been taken to the unknown against Davey Dolan but don't believe I tired much as the contest wore on, I was in pretty good nick and was still able to do some good ringwork as the contest progressed, Norton would not have fazed me I'm sure.

We had to go back to the drawing board though with Norton losing to Williams and I ended up facing a ticking-over contest, a local affair, against Darlington's Chris Burton, in Aberdeen.

Not to worry, I had a job to do and, although it was scheduled for ten rounds, I stopped him in just two. All that way for two rounds, it's a good job I got paid for this malarkey that's for sure. Then it was announced I'd got a shot at the English title, against Blackpool's Matty Askin.

It was around this time, late 2011-early 2012 that Lewis Pendleton, Ronnie Rowe and company were looking at an expansion of the Birtley ABC. Originally homed in Birtley's old Fire Station, remembered for the old shower block and lovely odours, Pendleton et al went for a re-location, and an impressive upgrade.

He added: "My first proper involvement with Ronnie was when we started looking at and raising money for a new home for the Dickinson's.

"When the new build for Birtley had opened, that was when I became more involved. That was when Frank had the lads and Ronnie and Gary were training them."

The Conditioning of Champions

Tyneside and the North East of England on the whole, have always produced athletes of top quality. In recent years those champions have seen their skills honed even further by the increasing presence of professional strength and conditioning coaches. They are seen as being the elite training personnel who can bring that added expertise to an athletes' regime.

But what is strength and conditioning and what role does such an individual provide?

It is seen as being the continuing development for elite athletic performance of both the physiological and physical attributes from within the individual. The coach, in this case Martin Nugent (Gateshead College Academy for Sport), provides the crossover between the applications of theory to the application of training. Within the strength and conditioning of an athlete a number of development attributes are looked at, and on a regular basis. They are now seen as being very much an integral part of athlete's coaching team and work alongside the other coaches in making the athlete the best that they can be.

The athlete(s) are therefore tested in relation to the sport in which they compete as well as their individual needs. The role of the strength and conditioning coach is to therefore see them develop that of 'The Complete Athlete' through the continued enhancement of their physical and physiological attributes. Examples of what the coach will look to enhance and work upon within the athlete includes that of Strength Development, Injury Prevention, Speed and Power, amongst other areas.

In the case of Martin Nugent, he has numerous roles in and around the sporting world. One of the primary positions sees him as being an integral part of the coaching staff, alongside that of Ronnie Rowe and Gary Barr, of the British Cruiserweight champion, Jon-Lewis Dickinson, and his younger brother, the Light-Heavyweight, Travis Dickinson. Both of whom are boxers and come from the Birtley Boxing Gym on the outskirts of Tyneside.

Working with and alongside the Dickinson's has only come about in recent times but is something that has definitely benefitted all parties. When discussing his role within the Dickinson camp, Nugent said that "I have been working with Jon now for approx. 18 months. I was asked by Ronnie Rowe who coaches Jon-Lewis and Travis Dickinson, which in my mind is a mark of a great coach.

"Over this time Jon has had three fights. When I took Jon on board I looked at how he moves, his posture etc and also asked both Jon and Ron what areas they want to improve on.

"I then set about improving Joint Stability so that we can then move onto power and speed development; I also worked on functional strength and core strength."

Within that statement is something which several people in the sport have motioned that Jon-Lewis needs to work on, his power and speed attributes. Although it is an area they do work upon, it is not something which overly concerns, and rightly so considering the fighters in-ring record.

"To be fair Jon has both but we strive to carry on improving this as this is the way I work. He does have a biomechanical disadvantage due to being tall with long limbs but since I have been working with Jon he is now developing more power off the back foot, his jab has more venom and also his foot speed upper body movement is better, I never put a time scale on this we just keep working but I guarantee by the next fight you will see even more improvement as myself and Jon have plan and are extremely committed to his athletic development," added Nugent.

"Jon was very open to new ideas and openly admitted to never training like this before, between myself and Ron we put together effective training camps that managed Jon well without "over training" which is a major issue in boxing ."

With those in mind Martin Nugent continued by discussing an example of a training camp which a champion of Jon-Lewis' stature is put through.

"In the last camp we worked in 4 week blocks starting with; Functional (movement) strength/Injury prevention work; Strength – moving into Olympic lifting technique; Power Development; and that of Fight Specific Fitness- endurance.

"An example of a week towards the later stages of the camp in endurance I would look to get Jon as lactic as possible working in circuits for three minutes with one minute recoveries, with also flexibility and joint stability sessions followed by ice bath treatments to aid with muscle recovery."

Not only in the pugilistic world does the talents of Martin Nugent's strength and conditioning come in though. "I have worked with numerous athletes from different sports, at the moment I currently work in Football working with Academy players from all three North East top clubs, and I also provide S & C support for the new, Houghton Kepier Elite Football Academy with ex-Sunderland player and Middlesbrough Reserve team coach, Martin Scott and alongside the Gateshead College Academy," Nugent imitated.

"I have also, within the last year, been made the Regional Strength Coach for the RFL (Rugby Football League) for which I work with talent identified, Rugby League players from around the region, and will be working with the England Development squads this year.

"On a weekly basis I also work within the sports of Golf, Cricket, and Judo and have just been asked to work with Talent ID, GB swimmers within the North East."

With so many different sporting ventures open then it can surely be difficult to be able to differentiate between the potential needs of individual athletes. Comparing those roles though was broken down when Nugent said that "The biggest difference between each sport really comes down to the mentality of the athletes more than the technical side of my job, for example Rugby players and boxers/ judo tend to be the most disciplined when it comes to the gym.

"You have to adapt your approach so that each athlete buys into the idea of strength and conditioning as this can be different, you really have to find out what will motivate them."

Recently it was mentioned that 'Every athlete should always have areas of development otherwise they become complacent,' to which Nugent provided greater insight into, saying that "if you ask any top athlete, past and present, and, if they are honest, they will tell you an area of their game they or always spend extra time working on, whether its technical or physical.

"To be a top athlete you need to commit every day to improving and getting closer to your overall goal each day, even if it is just an hour you could spare use that hour effectively. For example, if your flexibility is lacking then use that hour for that; or if you're a golfer and you need to work on your short game, or even a boxer who needs to improve power. This is something I try to imbed in everyone I work with.

"It is said you need approximately 20,000 hours training development to make it in sport."

In addition to all this, Martin Nugent has delved into the realms of Exercise and Nutrition in Sport and with this he continued by saying that *"I have worked in a personal training capacity but with a difference, as most PT's are what I call Health & Fitness based I bring in athlete performance based training "come and train like an athlete.*

"I also provide advanced Nutritional Testing to determine the nutritional ratios that will boost energy levels, improve sleep, sport performance and general wellbeing. This can help the body to gravitate towards the body's natural weight and body fat percentage."

Having also see his roles take him abroad to the USA (working in and around their developing Soccer environment) and in Spain (working with tri-athletes), Nugent is also employed, primarily, the Gateshead College Academy for Sport, where he is the head of S & C. With this Nugent concluded that *"I organise and manage the strength & conditioning team and the athletic development program. We have a state of the art Strength Performance Gym/ Performance Laboratories/Contrast bathing and indoor training facility. We work very closely with The English Institute of Sport.*

"We have up to 400 athletes from numerous sports. We also work with external teams and athletes and examples of this are; the RFL, Newcastle Eagles (Basketball), Gateshead FC, Newcastle Falcons (Rugby Union), Gateshead & Whickham Swimming Club, and England Judo."

(The above interview with Martin Nugent was first published in January 2011 and can be seen here - https://insidemannmedia.wordpress.com/2013/01/11/the-conditioning-of-champions/)

SEVEN

English Champion

KELLIE MALONEY, WHO WAS JON-LEWIS' manager and promoter until three-quarters of the way through his British title reign, said of the Dolan and Askin contests: "Dave Garside and company were very easy to work with and they wanted the fight with Jon-Lewis big time (for the Northern Area).

"I think Dolan was coming down from the heavyweights so we felt that he wouldn't be too strong, that and we had immense confidence in Jon-Lewis as well.

"At that time, to me, I was still managing an undefeated fighter (I don't class the injury reversals as losses) and Jon-Lewis was taught to fight at long range because of that jaw injury he had sustained (against Turba).

"He gave Dolan a boxing lesson and he could do that with people but there was also that thing in him, that he always wanted to prove himself and get involved in wars.

"After the Dolan win there was a lot of political moves going on but Jon-Lewis went and took the English challenge (against Askin) and won."

Two months after I'd taken care of Chris Burton up in Scotland I was right back in the thick of things.

I'd had a little time off after I'd beaten Dolan for the Area title but was now at the end of a second training camp in quick succession , why, because I'd been afforded the opportunity to challenge Blackpool's Matty Askin, who was Central Area champion and a thirteen-fight undefeated fighter at the time, for the then vacant English title.

He actually beat a future opponent of mine, Neil Dawson, for that Central cruiserweight title so credit to him for that, and he'd done reasonably since we clashed at the Oldham Sports Centre in April 2012 (it was the same show in which Anthony Crolla and Derry Mathews went to war for six rounds).

Askin was unlucky when challenging the Pole, Kryzsztof Glowacki for the WBO Intercontinental title what, seven months later as well whilst also losing, via majority decision, to Ovil McKenzie (more on him in a bit), but he's also won a few titles and could well become a decent champion having lifted the English, and British titles whilst also achieving something I didn't, defeat Tommy McCarthy (Askin inflicted defeat on him on Manchester in November 2016).

Myself and Matty, we already knew each other anyway and this contest was an interesting challenge, especially as I not only went in injury-free, but also had a strength coach in my locker, we'd recently added martin Nugent.

Being injury-free was actually a rarity for me going into title fight!

Even looking back, now, this was a tough fight for me, especially after Dolan and Burton so, with this also being a ten rounder I had to kind of approach things in the same manner – I trained for going ten rounds, for a fight, a war, and you go in there and do whatever you have to do in order to get the win.

Everything had been turned up a notch as well, very much so.

Running, pad and other gym work, sparring, even my dietary and conditioning requirements were taken care of and we all know what my diet is like, chicken and pasta, chicken and rice. These days that's completely out the window though.

People can certainly see, on social media, what my diet is like now, but during a fight camp, during my boxing career, whilst getting ready to face people like Matty Askin, then it was the chicken's, pasta's, steaks, a proper athlete's diet. A treat for me would be a chow mein.

There's always been some kind of logic to my craziness though that's for sure.

At the end of the day though you can only beat whoever is put in front of you and, although I wanted to face the likes of Rob Norton, Enzo Maccarinelli, I knew I had to overcome Askin first and you can't look to far ahead because of what can, or can't happen.

You really can't take anything for granted though and it's like, when I faced Turba, I didn't expect to get a broken jaw and my career to be hanging in the balance as it was, that could have been it right there and then.

As it turned out, the night against Askin was what dreams are made of for me, but for him it was a nightmare and I recall that, when Ronnie and me were driving over there in the car, heading across the A1, the song, 'Search for the Hero' came on the radio.

We both started singing it, loudly, and laughing away as we did and I was massively pumped up and ready to fight there and then; and we shared a big, king-size bed that night as well, it's how we rolled.

Having gone the full ten with Dolan though I knew I had enough in me against Askin as well and your body, no matter how much it hurts, you do get used to doing that much work.

Everything that I had done in training was spot on although Askin did have some power in him, that much was obvious and still is sis years on.

From early on though I realised that he was actually letting his shots go and it showed more as the contest progressed.

We'd worked a lot on my defence in training, hey I'd not that long come back from having my jaw cracked open, you don't, you can't, leave things to chance so that was kind of me taking away, stripping back any attributes he may have had going in against me and, once that happened, then proceedings became more comfortable for me as it got into the latter rounds.

The fight was on the undercard of Crolla-Mathews clashing for the British and I'm sure that, the more ours carried on, the more Askin didn't want to be in there, becoming jaded after what four, maybe five rounds and it's because of that the fight changed direction, in my favour.

I led from the beginning though, I set the pace and took most of what Matty threw at me, he mostly catching my gloves and arms before it ending up at the judges' scorecards, referee Phil Edwards affording the result in my favour with a 98-93, 97-93 (x2) whilst the main event saw Dirty Derry score a sixth round stoppage success over Million Dollar Crolla.

In all honesty, a fight like this , between myself and Askin, could have easily and should have been for the British title instead – two talented fighters as we were at the time with similar, but contrasting styles, deserved a much prize.

A lot of people enjoyed our fight and rightly so and I'm pleased he carried on and had the career which he has done.

(Askin would claim the English cruiserweight in 2012 against China Clarke, then again in 2016 when opposing Simon Barclay before lifting the British himself with an impressive seventh round stoppage of Craig Kennedy in May 2017).

COLLISION COURSE: Dickinson and McPhilbin collide for cruiserweight success

Looking back at the respective careers of these two, very different, pugilists, it soon becomes obvious that maybe, just maybe, their careers were due to collide at some point. For Jon-Lewis Dickinson (11-2; 3KO's) and Shane McPhilbin (8-3; 5KO's) clarity arrives in the form of results and both records are similar in nature, even competitively there are similarities.

Both were born just a few months apart back in 1986 but at opposite ends of our great country. Both made their professional debuts within months of each other as well, just in different weight divisions as McPhilbin began as a Heavyweight with a victory over Michal Skiemiewski (TKO4) in May 2009 and Dickinson has moved his way through the Cruiserweight ranks from the off, defeating Paul Bonson (PTS4) in November 2008.

The similarities don't end there either.

Both have appeared in the Prizefighter Series in the same year as Dickinson won the Cruiserweight one in April 2010 defeating Nick Okoth (KO3) in the final after success over Leon Williams (SD3) and Mark Krence (RTD1). McPhilbin on the other-hand was a beaten semi-finalist in the Heavyweight version in October later that same year, losing to Michael Sprott (UD3) having defeated Declan Timlin (TKO2) in the quarters.

Then there is the Regional Area titles both fighters have been successful in gaining as Dickinson took the Northern Area with PTS10 success over Sunder-land's David Dolan in July 2011 at the Stadium of Light. McPhilbin's was a much shorter affair though as he defeated Coventry's Rhys Davies (TKO3) in what was his opponents' last outing. Their impending collision in the Liverpool Arena on Saturday 13th will be over a mammoth twelve rounds.

And so the comparisons continue. But when that bell does go at the start of the first round all that comparison will be thrown aside; and two talented pugilists will go head to head for the chance to become the British Cruiserweight champion on the undercard of the 'Battle of the Olympians' between David Price and Audley Harrison. Price and Harrison will be competing for Price's British and Commonwealth Heavyweight titles.

It will be the first time that Dickinson will have attempted to traverse as many rounds whereas McPhilbin's last two bouts were conducted on twelve, against Leon Williams and Enzo Maccarinelli. However, Dickinson approaches this clash the same way he has previous bouts and stated "I've managed ten rounds without any bother, done them and can cope with this no bother as well."

McPhilbin was more forthcoming and said that "he (Dickinson) is a tall, fit lad and will have been training for a twelve round affair but I don't think that he is capable of being a one punch knockout.

"I like to get in and scrap and I think that, like me, he will fight anyone that is put in front of him.

"He, like me, will be looking at this fight and this alone before going further."

Between them both fighters have put in some hard yarns in their recent outings, and at the highest level. Dickinson went the full ten rounds with David Dolan and then Matty Askin last time out and, although McPhilbin has only had four rounds at Cruiserweight since stepping down from Heavyweight, his last three, including a six rounder with Simeon Coever, have gone the distance.

The last two for McPhilbin have been twelve round outings when defeating first Leon Williams (TKO12) to claim the British Cruiserweight title at the first time of asking. Then, in his last outing back in March, there was the controversial defeat to Enzo Maccarinelli (UD12).

"The winner from this clash will be in line for a showdown with Tony Conquest and then no doubt Europe and beyond," added McPhilbin.

The presence of Conquest's mention is something which relates to Dickinson and the fact that McPhilbin has got so far, so quick. With that Dickinson added "I had never heard of him until he faced Leon Williams.

"I've fought and earned my place whereas McPhilbin got lucky when Conquest dropped out of the bout with Williams. I can't blame him though for being fast tracked."

The British Cruiserweight title itself has been competed for since 1985 with its first holder, Sammy Reeson defeating Stewart Lithgo (PTS12) in Wandsworth, London. The North East's very own Glenn McCrory held the belt in 1988 and defeated both Tee Jay (PTS12) and Lou Gent (TKO8), the latter being at the Gateshead Leisure Centre. Other holders include Johnny Nelson, Terry Dunstan, Mark Hobson and Rob Norton. Two of Norton's British Cruiserweight title bouts were against Sunderland's David Dolan, a former opponent of Dickinson (when Dickinson won the Northern Area title).

(The above article is a combined piece on Dickinson versus McPhilbin, and was first published in October 2012 via https://insidemannmedia.wordpress.com/2012/10/13/collision-course-dickinson-and-mcphilbin-collide-for-crusierweight-success/)

EIGHT

Rule Britannia

MY BRITISH TITLE reign was probably the best twenty months of my boxing career from its beginning in October 2012 when I saw of the challenge of 'Mr Block,' Shane McPhilbin, through a rematch with David Dolan, a stern test against Mike Stafford, then fighting for keeps at Newcastle's Metro Radio Arena, against Neil Dawson in March 2014, who I stopped in ten,

That run would make me the only fighter to win all domestic honours, and in order; our Travis was a little unlucky in his pursuit of domestic honours but he also won the Prizefighter and English himself, at light heavyweight.

It's the British title, that lovely Lord Lonsdale belt, which means so much to any British fighter in any weight class from the lightest, flyweight, all the way up to the heavyweight.

Winning the British was always a dream for me, it was something which I aspired to achieve when I was but a lad, that and then a world title of course.

You learn very early on what the most important titles on offer are, everything else is just a bonus. It was then, when I was what, 15-16-years-old, and having thoughts about turning professional, that I realised that the biggest was winning a British title so, here I was, a decade or so later, with a chance of taking that first step towards achieving that goal and having to overcome (Bulwell) Nottingham's Shane McPhilbin (article prior to this chapter affords a little insight to the fight).

At the time I'd won eleven of thirteen contests and he'd notched up eight wins in eleven and was also of championship-winning stock as well having lifted the Midlands Area (2011) and the British (2012) cruiser-weight titles as well as having competed in the Prizefighter tournament, he being in the 2010 edition where he was a semi-finalist, losing to Michael Sprott.

I guess we were both relative unknowns prior to our respective Prizefighter tournaments so us meeting for the British was, I guess, inevitable really, and it was on live television with Boxnation broadcasting the fight on October 23 2012.

Other than fighting for the British title that's what I was looking forward to the most, fighting in front of a live television audience and boy did we make sure we were ready for it as well.

We'd been given plenty of notice that I was to challenge McPhilbin for the vacant title after Maccarinelli had been made to vacate it having defeated McPhilbin for it in the summer.

I'd have loved to have faced the Welshman, he being a former European and World champion, and he posed no real threat to me if I'm honest but decided to drop down a division and trade at light heavy instead.

That left the door open for myself and McPhilbin, Matty Askin, David Dolan, Tony Conquest and a few others, and yes, even to a bit point, Herbie Hide, who claimed to return at our weight at that time.

It would fall to Shane and I to have the first chance to dance and we'd been afforded a good three months' notice with it, twelve weeks for us to prepare for what was, at the time, the biggest fight of my career.

We had plenty of time to train, to prepare for it and, in doing twelve rounds I knew it would be different somewhat to previous outings, and a little more difficult as well.

I'd navigated the ten rounds against Dolan and Askin without any major problems so I knew that I wouldn't have any real problems in adding another two rounds to the equation.

Although the fight with Askin was some seven months prior, I didn't want another fight between with knowing that the British was next.

I'd never heard of him (McPhilbin) though until he faced Leon Williams and, to me, he got lucky gaining a title shot whereas I'd fought and earned my place at the top table. The results against Wright and Turba withstanding, I'd won every bout coming into it as well as having claimed three titles; McPhilbin on the other hand got lucky as Tony Conquest had dropped out in facing Williams leaving the door open for him to step in, I don't blame him for that though.

McPhilbin though, for me, was similar to Dolan in size and stature, Dolan also kept coming at me, McPhilbin has a got a solid punch to him and swings when trying to get through the guard. I knew that, if I kept my guard tight and worked round that, dominated using my strength and rhythm, and had the belief, then I'd achieve the first step towards achieving my dream.

And that's exactly what I did.

I'd overcome McPhilbin in twelve, sold rounds of non-stop boxing which to me, showed my abilities on the bigger stages, referee Steve Gray calling a unanimous decision result after the judges gave out a 118-110 (x2), 117-111 score.

McPhilbin had a varied career in the paid ranks winning the Midlands Area and British titles at cruiserweight whilst challenging for the Area at heavyweight. When opposing Dickinson it would be his twelfth of an eighteen-bout career.

Looking back at his clash with Jon-Lewis for the British title, and his own time in the sport around that period he said: "It (the title fight) doesn't seem that long ago.

"I'd fought (Enzo) Maccarinelli beforehand and lost the title but down to a few issues which he had, then had to relinquish it – I honestly feel I could have owned that belt outright myself (Dickinson was his third successive contest challenging for the British).

"However, prior to facing the Welshman I'd lost my trainer and don't think I fully recovered so my facing Jon-Lewis was something of an anti-climax really.

"Training went well and was away for a few weeks with the 23 Pioneers in Oxford, but mentally I wasn't right and the better man won on the night.

"Although we'd never met earlier I remembered him from his amateur days and I feel that, looking back now, I should have boxed differently. I knew I was frustrating him, he told me that during the fight, but I couldn't get it together and nothing was working for me.

"You live and learn though and I walked straight into his game-plan which proved costly; I should have walked away for a bit after the fight but never – fortunately I have a love for the sport back now.

"The one thing that stands out for me though is that, at the weigh-in, I had to run off an extra pound in weight so never really got up close to him until we faced each other in the ring on the night, that's when I realised someone has a nose as bad as mine.

"Seriously though, he always knew the score and was a very respectable, polite bloke."

THE NEXT IN line was the re-match, back on nearby Wearside, well at the Rainton Meadows Arena, in a Tyne-Wear derby with my old foe, David Dolan.

It had been nearly two years since I'd beaten Dolan for the Northern Area title and here we were, dancing again a north-east ring, this time opposing each other for my British cruiserweight title in the first defence.

Since our first meeting I'd gone out and defeated Burton, Askin and McPhilbin winning English and British titles, Dolan meanwhile only had two four round contests against Tayer Mehmed and Simeon Coever. Now here we were, in February 2013, meeting again and I wanted to go in that ring this time around a make a massive statement, make the boxing public sit up and take notice of me and recognise that I was in fact one of the best fighters in the country.

I wasn't prepared to take anything for granted though, I never did no matter who it was I was facing. There was a factor that went in my favour against Dolan in that it had been some time since he had gone that kind of distance in the ring whereas I had done, but I knew what he was like, the kind of fighter he was, and how prepared he and his team would have been, and that we both would have done a hell of a lot of work in the gym.

My build-up to facing Dolan the second time around was as intense as they come with sparring coming from all quarters in local amateur lads Simon Pendleton, Lawrence Osueke and Dean Laing, as well as pros such as the big Scotsman Gary Cornish, who was fighting on the undercard, and old friend China Clarke as well, he was preparing to face Wadi Camacho for my old English title around the same time.

(Cornish stopped Croat Jakov Gorpic in four rounds whilst China defeated Wadi Camacho on March 9 2013).

My getting in the ring and sparring with people of that calibre helped me with my speed and endurance, I got more used to the longer rounds as we continued pushing through the barriers.

I certainly needed it though because you think you've put in plenty of work during camp prior to a fight and you always go into every contest in the same way.

Back in February 2013 Maloney said prior to Dickinson – Dolan II that: "Dickinson versus Dolan is to be one of the best local derbies put together in a long time and better than some that Newcastle United and Sunderland put out."

All told it was a dangerous fight, more as it was probably a last-chance salon effort from him, if he lost to me, which he did, then he would in effect have nowhere left to go and that's what made it as good a fight as it actually was.

I wasn't relinquishing my belt and he had to go out there and beat me but, as it turned out, it was to be his last fight as a professional boxer.

After facing Jon-Lewis Dickinson, opponent David Dolan said: "My last twelve was probably against (Rob) Norton back in 2010 and I knew that was very close, there wasn't much in it.

"I also knew it was going to go the distance and he just seemed to be flicking shots that were getting scored but he never really landed; I do feel he nicked it though and all the times I've challenged for titles, they've been really close."

68

It was different though if I'm honest as most of my fights had been away from home with only three having been in the region; Turba, Wright, and the first Dolan fight.

The second fight with Dolan was brilliant and the kind of fight in which I always wanted to be involved with because I enjoyed a good battle, a good scrap, when I got between those ropes.

I do recall hurting my right hand midway through the fight but I was controlling the contest anyway, it would just make things a little awkward for me.

Looking back though, the fight with Matty Askin for the English title was an important one for me and I rate him one of the best in the country, he still is some four years on. The fight with him should have been for the British title but it was a good fight, not just for me but also for all those who watched it.

Dickinson or Dolan to reign at Supremacy

"Dickinson versus Dolan is to be one of the best local derbies put together in a long time and better than some that Newcastle and Sunderland put out."

That was how big time boxing promoter, Frank Maloney, of Frank Maloney Promotions, opened Thursday's press conference at the impressive Rainton Meadows Arena in County Durham, And, with that of Pro Boxing North East's Phil Jeffries sitting aside Maloney, the regions press and Loaded TV rolled up to bear witness to what was the British Cruiserweight face-off.

That is the main, headline bout, as Birtley's Jon-Lewis Dickinson (12-2; 5KO's) puts his coveted Lonsdale, British Cruiserweight title, on the line, with Sunderland's David Dolan (16-4-1; 5KO's) on the night of February 15th.

Alongside the main event duo was an impressive array of regional talent that were accompanied by the imposing presence of Gary 'Highlander' Cornish (12-0; 4KO's), who, as an undefeated pugilist and the chief support to the main event, has been in the north east for a few days sparring with the Cruiserweight champion, Jon-Lewis Dickinson.

Both Maloney, and co-promoter Jeffries, paid tribute to the welcomed presence of Sky's Loaded TV, with 'Supremacy' going out on the free-to-view, channel 200. Maloney welcomed their presence and stated that "we are hoping that this will be the first of many visits by Loaded TV to the north east and I'm not only delighted to have this on here, but to be able to with Phil (Jeffries) again."

Jeffries added to that by saying himself "myself and Neil Fannan are absolutely pleased to be putting this show on in the north east."

Following the introduction of the fighters, and with some questions being put to the Northern Area Lightweight champion Gary Fox, and the other duo in a derby, Peter Cope (holder of the International Masters Super Bantamweight) and his opponent David Lake, where a little, light hearted banter would ensue, the focus turned to that of Dickinson-Dolan II.

Both combatants find themselves at something of a crossroads in their respective Cruiserweight careers. Dickinson imitating that "it's something I've worked hard for all my life and the desire is definitely still there."

Dolan on the other hand found himself, and not for the first time either, taken back to the first meeting between the two in July 2011. With that in mind he added that "there wasn't much in it the first time around so we'll just have to see how this one goes."

Dickinson though insisted that "I am a better fighter than last time and you are going to see a better me.

"Yes there's more on the line now but I'm a hundred percent confident that I will keep my belt."

A late addition to the undercard saw the presence of Jon-Lewis' younger brother, light heavyweight contender, Travis Dickinson (13-1; 5KO's) whom narrowly lost to Bob Ajisafe for the English title in his last outing and is now looking to get back into the mix of things sooner rather than later.

Another two months passed after I'd defeated Dolan and we were up and at it again; I'm not sure I know how the other half put up with me during this period, I think I was constantly in the gym or fighting.

A second defence, and again at Rainton Meadows Arena, this time against Southport's Mike Stafford (he was 11-1; 2 at the time having made his debut back in 2006 and had fought Bonson, twice, Rasani, Anthony, Grainger during a stop-start career) – I could literally smell the dream, taste reality, feel success.

I knew that, in defeating Stafford, it would mean my next fight would be a date with destiny and the chance to own that beautiful belt outright and at this point, for me, Stafford was just another person that I had to beat, another fighter standing in my way of achieving a lifelong dream, so I just went in there and did what I had to do and hope that the end result went my way.

I guess that's why I sparred with China Clarke again, he helped a lot with the speed, and with local lad Danny Hughes, who was good for size and strength, and I trained for the full twelve so I knew that I had plenty in the tank.

What most people didn't know though, and I don't condone this behaviour either it's just I'm stubborn to myself, is that I went in against Stafford carrying an injury, I had deep tissue bruising on my pectoral muscles which ultimately meant that I couldn't throw my right hand at any great length and that's why I was seen to be fighting a more close range contest so yes, I was over the moon to come out of that fight with a win; Stafford certainly came up here to cause an upset.

It would have been a much better contest, from my perspective anyway, if I was fitter and had been able to throw punches properly.

The scoring of the contest was pretty accurate though, referee Victor Laughlin raising my hand in victory following a routine, unanimous decision score, 118-112, 117-112, 115-113, although I wasn't overly impressed with that third scoring of 115-113 but delighted to get the result I needed to chase the dream, destiny, and what a place to have it at as well.

Now an integral part behind the scenes, Lewis Pendleton was introduced to Maloney and team at the Rainton Meadows Arena ahead of the Stafford defence. It was then which Lewis had an inclination that the landscape was changing in the fight game, and in that of the Dickinson's.

"Having been introduced to Maloney at the Stafford fight I believe that it was apparent then that Frank was already having fought of retirement," Lewis continued.

"When Maloney eventually retired, releasing the likes of big Pricey, and Jon-Lewis, we were faced with a big decision as to what to do and I didn't know the fight game that well so I ended up spending quite a bit of time researching what it was all about.

"I quickly realized that I wasn't in a position to become a manager but Ronnie

was, ultimately he was the best person for that job and mine was to support him in a business capacity although I admit, we were rather naïve at the time as well.

"Fight deals were offered (Boxnation) and were looked at but they put clauses in them which, if they weren't met, he'd literally have been cast aside whilst the issue with me was the time it took for fights to even materialise, that and they wanted to co-manage him as well.

"None of this was in the best interest of Jon-Lewis, they even won the purse bids for the Dawson fight but the time elapsed on it and we were left running around looking for other options by which time Jon-Lewis had been out of the ring for some period which was when we came up with Fighting Chance Promotions – the lads having nowhere to train from.

(Fighting Chance saw the addition of a Gateshead Victoria ABC under the guidance of Steve Cranston).

"To me, in terms of facilities, we managed to build the second best gym in the region and that was good for me, it kept me sane – Jon-Lewis was the reason that that was put together and for the existence of Fighting Chance.

"I guess my regret was that Matchroom weren't as proactive in the region then as they are now and the odds were pretty much stacked against us so for us to be able to do what we did was great."

Other than the day I married my wife, Kate (9 August 2014) and the day we welcomed our gorgeous son, Joseph-Lewis (6 August 2015) into this mad, mad world, then 29 March 2014 is up there with the most important dates of my life for it was the night I went out and claimed the Lord Lonsdale belt for myself and, guess what, I did it in style, with a rare stoppage win, I couldn't have been happier.

I only stopped five opponents in my professional fight career – Nick Okoth, Mark Krence, Chris Burton, Neil Dawson, and Stephen Simmons, so the one against Dawson was especially sweet.

Doing it to win the British title outright, that last hurdle, and at the Metro Radio Arena, goose bumps and euphoria.

Dawson had a pretty decent record prior to facing me as well and arrived as the WBO International champion so I knew that, when he came up for Rotherham, he would come to do the same as me, leave it all out there in the middle of that ring. The only down side we both had was waiting so bloody long for the fight to actually materialise.

Between my beating Stafford, and facing Dawson, some eleven months passed, but I wasn't that bothered as I'd just had a few outings in quick succession anyway so the enforced break did me a lot of good really.

It was welcome relief as the injuries I was carrying in earlier fights were given time to heal properly; I'd had a perforated eardrum (McPhilbin), damaged hand (Dolan) and tissue bruising of the pectoral (Stafford).

There was also a rather unexpected setback as well as my then manager/promoter, Frank Maloney, took early retirement from the sport for personal reasons, they being that Frank became Kellie. It was a shock to say the least but we wish her all the best and thank her for all she did for the Dickinson name.

This meant that the roles in which Ronnie Rowe and Gary Barr had with me took on greater meaning, plus I had Martin Nugent (strength & conditioning), Chris Clayton (nutrition), and Lewis Pendleton around me as well as long-term stablemates in brother Travis, and the Birtley Bullet, Craig Dixon.

Maloney's decision was just that, Maloney's decision and I guess, when you think about it, I did start seeing changes from the person who both Travis and myself on back in 2008. Times move on though and Maloney realised that and, at the time, it was hard managing and promoting us two and we didn't know what was happening behind the scenes with Maloney.

That's when Ronnie stepped into management shows and Fighting Chance Promotions was formed with him and Lewis. I could have gone anywhere after Maloney but Ron had been by our side for years, as had Gary, so it made sense and I guess we owed them a chance to prove themselves as well, which they did.

When the fight finally came around, I just wanted to go in there and take him apart.

In the run-up to facing Dawson there was somewhat of an extra spotlight thrown on me due to events happening elsewhere involving other family members in the fight game so I'm actually glad I managed to complete what was a pretty decent hat-trick.

Our Travis had claimed the English light heavyweight title with a stunning stoppage success over Danny McIntosh then the following day my nephew Jacob reached the England schoolboy semi-finals, seeing Travis win though was absolutely brilliant.

It gives you that extra strength inside seeing each other doing so well, it helps to push you further and I just wished I wasn't as nervous for him as I am for me.

A highlight though was certainly visiting Newcastle United's cathedral on the hill, St. James' Park, showing off my title to the famous Toon Army (don't blame me but the Magpies lost 3-0 to Everton that night in front of some 47,622 fans); now that was blooming amazing and it's opportunities like that which don't come around all too often.

At the Arena though, it was my first time fighting in Newcastle as a professional boxer and to me there's no better venue than there. I'd watched other big fight nights at the same venue down the years, people like Audley Harrison (September 2001 against Dereck McCafferty on the Stephen Smith – Melikhaya August card), and the Joe Calzaghe/Ricky Hatton card a year later (December 2002 as Hatton defeated Joe Hutchinson for the WBU super lightweight and Calzaghe stopped Tocker Pudwill for the WBO World super middleweight).

My fight with Dawson was probably the most technically perfect contest of my career as a professional and I wore him down over ten rounds of a twelve round contest. I'd planned for a tactical battle with him, especially as he was known as being a dangerous fighter and had won twelve of his fourteen outings prior to getting in the Arena with me, so he'd proved his toughness during his career.

I was hoping to gain a stoppage success though, the fight being in front of my actual home crowd and not up the road, I had a lot of friends and family there, I needed a spectacle and with that prize at the end of it, well I couldn't have been happier.

Winning that meant everything to me and I'd caught him, dazed him, on several occasions during the fight. Early in the contest, yes he was a dangerous prospect, but I knew I had the strength and power to go the twelve so I had to make sure that I could take him further than he had been before, and wear him down whilst doing it, chipping away at him timing my shots throughout.

That fight proved that I was the best in Britain at cruiserweight.

I'd cleaned up domestically whilst overcoming some blips, injuries, and the departure of Maloney along the way.

After just five fights I'd gone into Prizefighter and upset the odds before going on to win the Northern Area, English, and British titles; I'd become unbeaten domestically for nearly three years since coming back from a broken jaw, and I wanted to move onto the European stage.

I'd achieved a dream of winning the Lord Lonsdale belt, the British title, outright, and was now able to keep it for myself, well, once I kept wresting it away from my mothers' clutches bless her, and the Boxing Board's as well for that matter as it really does hurt handing it back after every defence.

In defeating Dawson as comprehensively as I did, then I was able to own that belt outright, that's all that mattered, all that I wanted, to become the outright British champion and own the Lord Lonsdale belt.

Dickinson preparing for date with Destiny

There has been one goal spurring him on, that shining light at the end of what has been a long tunnel for one of the north-east's finest. For the night of the 22nd will see the Tyneside Cruiserweight king, Jon-Lewis Dickinson (14-2; 3KO's), that lifelong dream is the owning of the Lonsdale belt, outright.

Dickinson has but one more hurdle to overcome for that realisation to occur and will arrive on Tyneside in the shape of Rotherham's WBO International Cruiserweight title holder, Neil Dawson (12-2; 5KO's).

It has been some wait though for that final defence to be confirmed. This year just closing, 2013, began with the 27 year old Dickinson defeating local rival, David Dolan (UD12), for a second time, in February; then mandatory challenger Mike Stafford (UD12) in the April; both at Rainton Meadows.

Now though, the fighter who debuted back in 2008 with a PTS4 victory over Paul Bonson, is ready to take the next step up the ladder.

He said: "I'm more than looking forward to it and I think that our styles will definitely make for a good, hard fight.

"He (Dawson) is the type of fighter who will come and leave it all on the line, but I have that one last fight so I can keep the belt. Then nobody can take it off me."

Having been successful in claiming the 2010 Cruiserweight Prizefighter title, expectations were to be understandably high in the Dickinson camp. Successive losses though rocked and injuries sustained put Dickinson very much on the back foot. A change in tact would see him come back on the championship road.

In July 2011 David Dolan was beaten for the Northern Area strap and the proverbial bit between the teeth was back. Dickinson has been unbeaten since. Victories over (Chris) Burton and (Matty) Askin followed as Dickinson claimed the English Cruiserweight strap and a shot at the British title. Shane McPhilbin was on the receiving end as Dickinson was crowned British champion and the rest was, as they say, history. But it came not without a cost.

Dickinson added: "I'm not overly bothered that I have had to wait as long for this third defence as I had those two outings quick off the belt earlier this year.

"It has actually come as a welcome relief as well to be honest, the extended time off. The three bouts in seven months encapsulated an unlucky spell of injury as well. Against McPhilbin I had a perforated eardrum; then I damaged my hand before facing Dolan for the second time. When I faced Stafford I went in there with a broken rib. Now though we have a set date so we can focus on the job at hand."

Although there are still some three months until he appears at the Gateshead Leisure Centre, Dickinson and his team (Ronnie Rowe, Gary Barr and Martin Nugent), now based at the Gateshead College Academy for Sport, and are pretty much counting down the days. And, since the retirement in October of Frank Maloney, Dickinson, along with younger brother Travis and stable mate Craig Dixon, the trio find themselves managed by long-time mentor, trainer, and friend, Ronnie Rowe. It is a move that has been more than welcomed by the Tyneside trio.

Looking ahead to Dawson, Dickinson said, "I've just been doing bits and pieces in the gym and trying to keep myself ticking over really.

"I'm feeling really good about myself and find myself in the gym a few nights a week at present; I have been for a while. We'll get Christmas and New Year out of the way first then go full steam ahead into an eight week camp right up till fight night. It's all coming together nicely though."

The two main topics of immediate interest surround the announcement of the retirement of Frank Maloney and the signing with Ronnie Rowe, as well as the facing of Dawson, before pondering a future within the Cruiserweight division.

Dickinson continued: "It was his (Maloney's) choice to retire and the goings on behind the scenes would have helped move it more.

"I did start to see a change in him from when I turned professional back in late 2008. Times moved on though and he realised that. He was a likeable enough bloke and we got on really well with him but it was hard managing and promoting the both of us (Jon-Lewis and Travis) whereas Ronnie (Rowe) will just be managing us.

"I see this as being more a beneficial scenario as he will be looking out for us and going out there and getting what will be the best deals for us. I could have gone with anyone really but he (Rowe) has been with me for years now and it was the logical, the only choice, to make."

As for what could well be a twelve round war with Neil Dawson early next year, a distance for which the challenger has not yet traversed. The furthest Dawson has been is six and the last time that happened was in September 2012.

Dickinson picked up on that fact and stated: "I've certainly got the experience advantage over the longer rounds but I certainly won't be going in there thinking that he won't be fit enough, because he will be.

"I can do the twelve rounds, both in fighting and in sparring. I'm more than comfortable doing it and had invaluable experience with it as well. The Dolan fight was done at a hard, fast pace. I'm just going to go in there and take him apart.

"I certainly wouldn't have minded a few more stoppages on my record as I know that I can stop people but I know that now, going into fights, that I have that in my mind, that I can do it,"

In addition, a recent addition to the Cruiserweight ranks has caused some raised eyebrows. Former WBO Light Heavyweight champion, Nathan Cleverly, is looking to make waves, and fast. Cleverly not only offers food for thought but is also a challenge that the hungry Dickinson would savour.

"His (Cleverly's) arrival in the division is great, you can't deny that," Dickinson formulated.

"After I defeat Dawson I will be looking at moving on to the European and World stage and if Cleverly was to take the Commonwealth title then he and I would surely make for a great matchup later next year. I would also look at a possible clash with Ola Afolabi."

(Jon-Lewis Dickinson interview prior to the Dawson fight in December 2013, original interview via https://insidemannmedia.wordpress.com/2013/12/01/dickinson-preparing-for-date-with-destiny/)

NINE

Regrets & Injuries

EVERYBODY HAS regrets at some point in their lives, personally or professionally, the same with injuries as well, these coming around a lot more not only because I was athlete, but also because of my chosen sport.

This is the same both for regrets, and for injuries and man have I had a good few injuries in my career but I've never, and I mean never, used them as an excuse not to get into the ring and earn my living, not like some boxers do.

I've collected many an injury during fights, I've harboured a good few injuries during training camps, and I've battled through the pain even going into several title fights carrying an injury of some sort.

My jaw has been broken a couple of times, I've had my nose shattered, I've got big ears, oh is that not an injury, oh well, it is now hass! hass!

But I have always been a sexy beast, and yes, Kate agrees with that statement, as do the lads, so it never did me any damage did it...

Seriously though, injuries like that can affect people in different ways and not just with time out as well, I guess that it's just down to the individual and how they act and react to a situation, that and the kind of team you have around you.

My first major injury in the pros arrived in that fight against Richard Turba (September 2010) although I did have broken nose in the amateurs by the Irish champion, Alan Reynolds. That injury, a broken jaw, arrived in what was my second loss in the pros, I'd picked up another injury in the fight with Tyrone Wright as well.

I'd gone down in three against Wright a few months earlier and my next outing was scheduled to be a rematch with him, the fight having been made in the immediate aftermath of that loss. I did some pretty stupid things in the fight with Wright as well, I guess I got a little cocky which in turn led to my becoming rather complacent and I needed, wanted the rematch in which to put that right.

Well, it doesn't work like that now does it and what, maybe 72 hours before I was scheduled to rematch Wright, the game-plan changed dramatically and I was fighting Turba instead.

Those two didn't even stick around the pro game that long and only had twenty-five fights combined, and here's me losing to both of them in quick succession, talk about bum luck (Wright finished with a 9-4-2;4 record whilst Turba ended on 6-3-1; 5).

Now, looking back at the Turba fight, it did have a few positives emanating from what was a major negative, I mean, come on, I went into that fight and had my jaw pretty much smashed up in three rounds.

Although that was a horrific accident at the time, it would be for anybody really, I also think that actually became a blessing in disguise.

I'd trained for and won the Prizefighter earlier that year and had gone straight into pretty much two consecutive outings in my then ongoing quest to become champion and efforts like that do actually take their toll.

That broken jaw meant I was given some enforced time off and I still believe, even more now, that I matured and came back both mentally and physically stronger than I was prior to those fights and that the seven fight winning streak I went through over the next few years kind of justifies my thought process.

It gave me time to rethink, regroup, and with the injury coming early in the contest, it showed my strength of character to continue battling through such conditions and, the thing was, other than those close to me during the fights, people weren't aware.

So, what does a broken jaw do, what effects did it have on me, more as I have a loved of food and drink.

Well immediately after, in the hospital before the wiring and stuff was all fixed to me, and wearing those lovely gowns with me butt hanging out the back of it, I was chasing the nurses down the corridor at feeding time as I wanted to mash up my corned beef sandwiches with the soup and downing it all together – that was bloody lovely.

Basically it was straight up terrible to be honest and those first six weeks were horrendous, they really were, especially as my jaw was wired together and strapped up by an elastic band – worst of all, I couldn't bloody eat anything. Those who know me know that stopping me eating and drinking is actually a daft thing to do.

The mental and physical battles you have to overcome are actually rather crazy, and quite time-consuming to say the least; my weight started to drop off considerably and, for about six months, I was also fighting to get my licence back.

The boxing board are rather stringent at the best of times and rightly so considering the dangers and the challenges that this sport presents, but when coming back from injuries, especially like that, then it makes things a little harder.

The hoops you have to jump through, the obstacles you have to overcome, well let's just say that there's a few of them, but we, as a team, carried on pushing for my licence, writing regular letters to the Boxing Board requesting updates and having constant appointments with consultants at the hospital, making sure that everything was right.

It was a really hard time though as there's not much you can do yourself either, I couldn't even train much.

What's even more bizarre is that, when I was on that long road back to full fitness, I began helping our kid in his sparring sessions for his turn in the light heavyweight Prizefighter.

As soon as I was able to get back into the ring I did but what you all didn't know at the time is that he had taken a bad rib injury himself in sparring; he didn't want people to know about that we kept it between ourselves in the gym.

Therefore, with his not being able to get sparring anywhere else, I stepped in and sparred him under the premise that I wouldn't do any body shots if he did no head shots – we sparred a lot down the years, they were fun.

Another example was in my second British title defence at the Rainton Meadows Arena (April 2013) against Mike Stafford which I went into nursing an injury.

I'm too stubborn for myself though that's been the problem throughout my career but I'm not going to pull because of that kind of injury. A broken jaw is different but against Stafford it was 'only' a deep tissue bruise of the pectorals.

Yes, I know that injuries can be extenuated if not cared for correctly but I know that I also had a very important ten rounds ahead of me that I needed to get through.

Other people would have pulled out with lesser injuries though and I believe the adrenaline that was pumping through my veins covered it up rather good and again, only those that were close to me were aware of it, kind of like our kid had done with his rib injury prior to his Prize-fighter success.

There's no point in divulging these things prior to a fight either, it gives your opponent an advantage and shows a weakness in yourself, or you'll just end up pulling out.

I showed a lot of mental strength from within to overcome those injuries and still get in that ring and I'm proud of myself for showing that much willingness through adversity.

The main disadvantage to getting in there though is that you're unable to do your job properly and, as a professional boxer, it's a case of either punch or be punched, losing the ability, a percentage, of being able to do something, can prove detrimental and you have to then heighten the awareness of other senses in order to maintain yourself accordingly.

Aside from the injuries you've also got regrets as well.

Granted I'd gone on and won the British title outright but the losses

I succumbed to after defeating Dawson, against Ovill McKenzie and Courtney Fry, the first losing the British and challenging for the Commonwealth, those two hurt.

Against McKenzie, he was a big puncher and had stopped half of his opponents during his career (some notable stoppages on his record would include Tony Conquest, Enzo Maccarinelli, Tony Dodson and Jeff Evans).

The build-up to that fight was probably the least enjoyable I've had in the game as well and it's the only time really any feelings like that happened to me and I'd thought that, after beating Dawson and gained ownership of the Lord Lonsdale, I wouldn't be fighting until after I'd married Kate, which happened in early August 2014.

Because of that I'd put boxing on the back-burner in my mind as everything else was all booked up so looking back I should maybe have cancelled the stag do and the wedding, oops I mean not taken the fight. That's it, I shouldn't have taken the fight with McKenzie, more as I had less than five weeks to prepare for what essentially was a really big fight.

Come on, five weeks to prepare for a British and Commonwealth title contest with someone like McKenzie. I know I'm mad but, as I was due to get married as well, I'd just got back from Vegas. I think the drink may have got the better of me.

On the night of the fight itself it fast became like one of those bad sparring sessions and I just couldn't get myself going no matter how hard I tried, no matter what I did.

The fight against McKenzie is probably my biggest regret, and I'll never watch it back, I couldn't. I was horrible and still don't know what I was thinking.

I've seen the photos from the fight, that's enough for me. I tried to get to close to him and it didn't work, after all he's a world-class puncher and just didn't have it but I believe that, at any other time, I'd have beaten him comfortably.

He stopped me in two rounds, the quickest loss of my career and to then go out and lose to Fry, after my wedding, then thank the lord above for wedded bliss that's for sure.

At least the loss I had to McCarthy went the distance, even if it had some bad moments but things happen and what's life without injuries and regrets.

We are tested for a reason and the low points can, in turn, set me up for some significant high points as well, just look at me, seriously, I know you all want to look at my beautiful face hass! hass!

After the losses and injuries against Wright and Turba I went on that near four year unbeaten streak and winning all those titles.

After the losses to McKenzie and Fry I faced, and defeated, one of only three unbeaten fighters I opposed during my career, Stephen 'Simbo' Simmons.

Dickinson brothers aiming for some unfinished business at Geordie Roar

There's been some mixed emotions in the Fighting Chance Promotions camp in recent times.

New additions have added some much needed impetus to the trio already present, and they've had a rough time of late with all three, Jon-Lewis and Travis Dickinson primarily (Craig Dixon included), looking to rectify things on Saturday night.

When they step into the Metro Radio Arena they will be aiming to brush away some unfinished business that has no doubt been acting like a mill round their respective, bulging necklines.

Cruiserweight Jon-Lewis Dickinson had a mixed 2014 and he saw it capped by winning the Lonsdale belt outright (stopping challenger Neil Dawson in ten). For the elation that came with that he was soon brought back down by heavy-hitting Ovill McKenzie, which was soon followed by a shock reverse against Courtney Fry.

Now he is being afforded a third bite of the cherry as he steps into the international forum with a WBC International Silver title scrap with Scotland's undefeated Stephen Simmons, 11-0(5). It is, in all honesty, an opportunity he can't afford to let slip and he goes into it brimming with his usual confidence.

"We've had a lot of sparring going into this show," Jon-Lewis began as both he and younger sibling, Travis, have gone through a lengthy camp together.

"Not only have we had some great sparring with the likes of Matty Askin, Lawrence Osueke, Simon Pendleton and Declan Fusco, but we had a great spell in Ireland again. Add the fact Travis and I have been toe-to-toe again then it's all good. "

With Travis, he also makes his international bow when he opposes Spaniard Mustafa Chadlioui, 5-1-1(3), over eight rounds. The Tyneside light heavyweight has also endured some mixed fortunes of his own and, had it not been for fiasco and injury surrounding Bob Ajisafe and the MaxiNutrition finale, would surely have been British champion by now.

"Ajisafe is done with for now," claimed Travis as he talked of the rawness which overshadows recent altercations between the two.

"If he has a title though and I want it, then we'll see. Now though it's about Chadlioui and my taking care of him. To me he looks like he can only work things on the inside whereas I will be bringing the power game with me so we'll see how long he lasts on Saturday night really."

Both fighters will be hoping for several outings this year as they progress up their respective divisional world rankings and, as they step into the ring side-by-side, the Dickinson brotherhood has never been so strong.

Unfinished business they most certainly have, and for different but contrasting reasons.

(Brief interview with Jon-Lewis and Travis Dickinson prior to Geordie Roar, April 2015 via https://insidemannmedia.wordpress.com/2015/04/02/dickinsons-to-clear-up-some-unfinished-business/)

Prizefighter tournament & winner

Brother Travis
also becomes
Prizefighter
champion

'Cobra-time'
Jon-Lewis &
Travis with 'The
Cobra' Carl Froch

Northern Area
champion vs.
David Dolan

English
champion after
defeating
Matty Askin

Pose-down
ringside with
Jon-Lewis

It's mine!
- British
champion with
Barrzy &
The Dish

Jon-Lewis wins WBC International Silver with stoppage of
Stephen Simmons @ Metro Radio Arena

Jon-Lewis wins British outright vs. Neil Dawson
@ Metro Radio Arena

TEN

Taking Simbo's Strap

PRIOR TO THE SIMMONS FIGHT, Jon-Lewis Dickinson suffered consecutive losses, to Ovill McKenzie and Courtney Fry, both under differing circumstances. It was, in all aspects, not the kind of start Fighting Chance had expected, more as Jon-Lewis had been crowned British champion outright.

A lot was happening behind the scenes as well, with some big names being mentioned as potential opponents for the elder Dickinson, Lewis saying:

 "We couldn't stop Jon-Lewis from fighting (McKenzie) to which afterwards, with what happened, we'd effectively retired him there and then, but had a look at (Courtney) Fry.

"*Boxnation had offered Jon-Lewis, of all people, Oleksandr Usyk, abroad in the Ukraine but at a few weeks' notice, and we all knew that he'd have taken it given half a chance; we took Fry instead and used the show (Resurrection) as the launch of Fighting Chance.*

"*That night, all three of our fighters lost (Craig Dixon to lee*

Mould for the Area title, and Lewis Scott), although it was a great show.

"What happened next is that we were all really upset and deflated, understandably so. Nobody expected Fry to come out and fight how he had done and do what he did to Jon-Lewis.

"In the midst of all this we were offered a fight with one of Jon-Lewis' heroes, Roy Jones Jnr (an American light heavyweight/cruiserweight/super middleweight/middleweight who had a stellar fight career finishing with a record of 66-9; 47, cleaning up the light heavyweight division ta one point holding the IBA, IBF, IBO, WBA, WBC and WBF World titles whilst also lifting both the WBU and WBC cruiserweight straps; he's known as being the first fighter to inflict defeat on the Jackie Kallen-managed, James Toney, for the IBF super middleweight strap in November '94 with his first word title coming against Bernard Hopkins, at middleweight, the year before) whilst Matchroom came to the table with Stephen Simmons so out thought process was that, he beats Fry then faces Simmons, but he lost and we thought those opportunities were gone.

"Ronnie goes off on one of his fishing trips to the Gambia so is out of contact big time and the next I know, Jon-Lewis is coming in to see me in the office at work, telling me he messed up on a few things in the build-up to Fry, some things were right, but he wanted Simmons and could I contact (Eddie) Hearn.

"I'm scared of the Dish as it is so here's me thinking, right, he's away for three weeks, and what am I going to do. We'd all spoken and felt it had been the end of Jon-Lewis (after the Fry defeat). I was bricking it and thought, that's it, my friendship with Ronnie is done, and he's going to kill me.

"I took a gamble with that fight and I'm pleased it paid off and I didn't want to be put in a position like that but for me, other than the birth of my daughter and my wedding, the night against Simmons was the best night of my life."

It was the night I was expected to get back into title

contention, to take Simbo's WBC International strap and start opening up those bigger doors for me.

In a way, although I won, you could say that things didn't quite transpire how they were supposed to for me, then again, do they ever?

Having won the British outright at the same venue, the Metro Radio Arena, thirteen months earlier, on what was, at that time, the greatest professional moment of my life, I actually went into the ring against the uneaten Scotsman (Simmons had won eleven straight prior to opposing Dickinson and claimed the WBC International Silver title with a tenth round stoppage of Wadi Camacho in Glasgow, June 2014) on the back of two straight losses, against Ovill McKenzie and Courtney Fry, both of which were tough fights and for differing reasons.

It wasn't the first time I'd lost two-in-a-row though, the same had happened four years earlier as well after I'd won the Prizefighter, losing to Wright and Turba in quick succession.

Therefore, going into this clash with Simmons, I wasn't fazed as I'd experienced similar situations before in my career and it's right what promoter Eddie Hearn had said beforehand as well, this was, in all honesty, a must-win fight for me and, after the recent two losses, beating Simmons showed that I still belonged at the top level.

My fighting Simmons, it was a fight that I had wanted for a long time, prior to Hearn and Matchroom announcing they were coming back to Newcastle. When we heard that this show, 'Geordie Roar,' was going to happen the first thing I did was get onto Ronnie and Lewis and told them I wanted to have that fight, at the Arena.

Bizarrely, as things actually transpired, Simmons and his time actually beat me to the punch and they were already offering us the fight; it was the only time he'd beat me to the punch and I bet they regretted it the following day.

The style of fighter in which he is, that's the style that I've like opposing if I'm honest, it brings out the best in me as a fighter. Don't get me wrong here, he's a great bloke with a good track record before he faced me; he was undefeated and a former GB squad member, plus he was a title holder. Accolades of that distinction aren't easy to ascertain, they are earnt, over time.

But, we'd watched him a lot and the more we looked him and what he brought to the ring, the more we realised that he wasn't that hard to hit and I'd just need to go in there and stay the course longer than he did. I had power myself, although I rarely used it, so I knew that I was more than capable of doing a job that way as well so I just had to see what happened when we both got into the ring.

It was certainly a do-or-die situation for me and we knew that he was a strong fighter, someone who would come forward, maybe enough to actually try and blast me out himself.

He will have looked at my previous two outings, against McKenzie and Fry, and thought exactly that, after all, the McKenzie fight finished early and Fry had put me on the seat of my pants during that contest.

This time around though there wasn't any trouble on my behalf and it showed throughout.

It was a great fight as well, not just for us being in it but for the fans watching both ringside and on Sky Sports.

Granted he kept closing the gap down well and landed some bloody good shots on me which meant I had to keep my range and try not to get myself dragged into an all-out brawl, that's the one thing in which we didn't want to happen.

It probably wasn't until the seventh round that the

contest started flowing more in my favour and I finished that one on top, starting the decisive eighth even stronger. The right, which I landed at the beginning of the eighth round, it was a pretty sweet shot and an even sweeter feeling and I knew myself, right then, deep down, that I'd got this, I just needed to pull out the exclamation point.

I'm sure the Arena erupted when I landed that right, then the left, which sent Simbo crashing to the canvas and it was a stupendously amazing feeling when referee Ian John Lewis called an end to the contest right then, giving me that WBC strap.

Both of us had predicted KO wins over the over prior to the fight and I'm lucky that it was mine that came to fruition and, although Simmons went on to have a further nine outings since we clashed, it wouldn't be too long that I would hang up those leather gloves.

What do I recall of the finish that night?

Relief more than anything if I'm honest, not just for me but for my team, my family and close friends. Most of us had been through a lot getting to this particular point so we were relieved that I'd gone in there, got the job done, and got the result which we wanted, needed.

You can see what a result like that meant just by looking at the reactions in the fight photos from the night, the look of sheer joy and pure elation not only etched across my face, but also on that of Barrzy and the Dish. I was something else indeed and that night, in defeating Simbo for the title, is one of those great memories for all of us.

It's just a shame that our Travis lost his contest or it would have been an even sweeter night but hey, he's had some pretty decent wars himself and did alright for himself and I guess it just wasn't meant to be against that Mustafa Chadloui bloke.

I honestly thought that, realistically, after I'd beaten

Simmons at the Arena, and don't forget I'd done so rather convincingly, I thought that something bigger was around the corner for me. Simmons was undefeated before he faced me and I took care of him in eight rounds.

We all thought that, after that, I'd be back out fighting again pretty quickly, get another good win or two under my belt, and then get a shot at revenge against Tony Bellew (at that time 'The Bomber' had not long since beaten the previously undefeated Welshman, Nathan Cleverly, on a split decision. It was a result which took Bellew's record to 23-2-1 and was the WBO International cruiserweight champion).

For me though it was, again, nearly twelve months before my next fight came about and that wasn't really good enough in the grand scheme of things. It wasn't down to lack of trying, more opportunities weren't presenting themselves or, if they did, they were at too short notice.

I think that a couple of fights fell through, for one reason or another, and nobody was willing to take a chance so, when I did finally get back into the ring, having participated in ten and twelve round contests for the majority of the previous four years, it was a meagre six rounder.

Czech journeyman, Jiri Svacina, would prove to be my eventual next opponent after Simmons. Granted he'd been in the ring with, and ultimately lost, to a few decent names before he face me, his previous four outings were against Tony Conquest, Stephen Simmons, Enzo Maccarinelli and Matty Askin, and he'd even fought for a few titles early in his career but then, at the point, he was a journeyman.

I'd not done that since 2010, that's how I felt, there was that same kind of feeling in me and that it was just a journeyman; it's always been hard for me to put to my mind to something when there's no challenge, no eliminator, no title on the line, no sense of progression. That's just how I am and that's how I felt it was, like when I turned professional and had those early fights.

As it turned out, the fight with Svacina, it went the full six rounds with referee Andrew Wright calling it 60-54 in my favour, but a lot had changed, both for and inside me and, although I fought Tommy McCarthy just two months after the Svacina fight, that was it, I was pretty much done and, in all honesty, my heart had gone, and I felt old in the ring, among other things.

Jiri Svacina, the fight of Jon-Lewis' career that most tend to forget, the win that became an anomaly and, in all honesty, wasn't supposed to happen as thoughts were on other opportunities which, as was the case in Jon-Lewis' career, failed to materialise, for one reason or another.

On this specific period Lewis Pendleton said:

 "Svacina wasn't actually supposed to happen, we were supposed to have Jon-Lewis against Craig Kennedy (Welsh fighter who claimed the IBF International strap against Joel Tambwe Djeko in May 2016 before losing a challenge for the English title against Matty Askin in June 2017) and I'd spoken to Barry McGuigan and Cyclone Promotions about the two meeting for the IBF International cruiserweight title.

"It was to be a home fight for Jon-Lewis then, three weeks into camp we get a call from Hearn after he'd impressed against Simmons.

"He (Simmons) was scheduled to oppose Tommy McCarthy but had pulled out with an injury had the boxing board had installed Jon-Lewis to fight McCarthy.

"We'd had an offer to fight on one of the Smith undercards in Liverpool but that was two weeks' notice; Bellew was being talked about as a potential opponent as well in a few fights and it was said that, if Bellew had won the world title a defence would be scheduled against Dickinson in Newcastle or Liverpool, but only if he'd stayed successful and relevant.

"The IBF was lined up against Kennedy, then Simmons is pulled from the McCarthy fight and Jon-Lewis is put in his place but we actually turned it down, it wasn't something we were interested in really but Matchroom were brilliant and had sourced and paid for Svacina.

"I believe that Jon-Lewis would have beaten Kennedy easily and would have probably gone on to face Bellew for the world title but instead he eventually faced McCarthy, and was gone."

Looking back on what had been a relatively successful career for Jon-Lewis, his mentor, coach, friend, general dogsbody, Ronnie Rowe summed it all up saying:

 "We've got some great memories and he enjoys living his life, but he was one hell of an athlete as well.

"The likes of Jon-Lewis, and Travis, did great, especially when coming from a village/countryside upbringing that they had and to come back, like he did in the amateurs after losing to Bellew, and to win an ABA title two years later, that was something else."

"Winning a Lonsdale belt outright was no easy feat," explained Kellie Maloney.

"I like the way in which I handled his career, and the way in which he fought during it.

"Would I have changed anything? I don't think so, and I always felt that he was capable of achieving what he did, maybe more."

Of the numerous highlights in the career of Jon-Lewis Dickinson, long time friend and trainer, Gary Barr, said:

> "Winning that British title outright and defeating Simmons, both at the Metro Arena, were special, standout moments for me.
>
> "They were definitely the ones right there."

Whilst The Dish added:

> "Personally, winning the Prizefighter was the one.
>
> "I was in a pro corner for the first time and to go through the changing of tactics, for three different fighter, in one night, was certainly something else.
>
> "Also, I agree with Barrzy, the victories over Dawson and Simmons, they were special indeed."

Jon-Lewis makes a Geordie Roar as he rocks Simbo for the title

He said all along that he would do it and how and, as the final blow landed during the eighth round Fighting Chance Promotions had a new cruiserweight champion.

Jon-Lewis Dickinson, 16-4(5) had proved all the doubters wrong and in some style after taking the fight to the now dethroned WBC International cruiserweight and lit up the Metro Radio Arena with an immense Geordie Roar.

Having suffered losses to Ovill McKenzie and Courtney Fry in his last two outings it was, in many people's eyes, the last chance saloon for the Tyneside cruiserweight, it was the last bite of a three bite cherry – he wasn't going to let it go, not on his life.

Upon entering the arena to a proper Geordie welcome afforded by the baying masses, Jon-Lewis and his corner, Ronnie Row and Gary Barr, set out the most perfect of game plans, and it was executed with precision.

From the opening bell it was vintage Dickinson as the 28-year-old cruiserweight rolled back the years and gave a performance to remember, utilising the inside to maximum, throwing the jabs, working the combo, and the footwork was just ideal. Simbo was just not at the races and Dickinson smelled blood.

When the soon to be dethroned champion did get some shots away Dickinson's guard held firm bar a few shaky moments when the duo traded blows late on. For Jon-Lewis though, the little showboating he caressed the crowd with in the fourth epitomised the class and level of fighter he now is.

Afterwards he said: "That was absolutely brilliant, it was a class atmosphere and the crowd were just great, they really were."

It was that crowd which Jon-Lewis fed off, their energy coming through every punch he landed on Simmons and he was confident with it as well. It was in the sixth though that proceedings were all in Jon-Lewis' favour after what was probably the most perfect round saw foot and handwork go through the gears with ease, and the crowd purred in appreciation.

"I just worked through it, made him miss a lot and slipped his jab," added Jon-Lewis. "When he did get in was when he was up close and I was a little messy and let him in but I controlled it well and didn't see any other outcome."

When the dust is settled, and the Dickinson camp take stock of all the emotions that came with an incredible Matchroom Geordie Roar, they will come to *realise that fighters like the Dickinson's, and the expectant Geordie faithful, is all that it cracked up to be.*

"The whole arena celebrating as they were was just the best thing," Jon-Lewis said with a wry smile. "At the end of that sixth, when I caught him (Simmons) with a few great shots, I could feel them roaring me on.

"Ron (Rowe) and Gary (Barr) were spot on during the fight and I couldn't have asked for any more from them. We have worked on a lot for the past two and a half months, on how we would do this, what we would concentrate on, and what I wanted to do in the bout and not him."

Jon-Lewis aside it was disappointment for younger brother Travis who was stopped in the first round of his comeback from injury against Spaniard Mustafa Chadlioui. As his elder bother said afterwards it sums up boxing completely.

"It's a great sport but it's a horrible sport at the same time." Amen to that!!

(Report and interview on Jon-Lewis Dickinson defeating Stephen Simmons first published in April 2015 via https://insidemannmedia.wordpress.com/2015/04/05/elder-dickinson-gives-a-geordie-roar/)

ELEVEN

Early Retirement?

I GUESS you could say that my career in boxing didn't exactly finish, not only how I wanted it to, hut how others, professional or otherwise, would have expected it to; mind they also say that all good things must come to an end.

With me, finishing my career was a combination of several things really and, even if I had defeated Tommy McCarthy at the SSE Hydro in Glasgow, I may still have ended up having to walk away.

Isn't it funny how life deals you with whatever hand it sees fit to do so? Well the McCarthy fight was seen in a similar vein as being one of those 'last-chance saloon' kind of fights.

I'd beaten Simbo, convincingly, for the WBC Silver over a year beforehand, it was similar to the gap between defeating Dawson and facing Simmons, after which nothing materialised for me, only that meagre six round affair with Jiri Svacina.

No disrespect to the kid (Svacina) but he's not somebody whom I'd have chosen at this stage of my career so, having lost the British (and Commonwealth) quite emphatically to Ovill McKenzie two years prior, here I was faced with an eliminator, over ten rounds, for, you guessed it, the British title, and against a young, hungry, up-and-coming, unde-feated Irishman.

Now I'm sure I can get an Englishman (myself), Irishman (McCarthy) and a Scotsman (Simmons) joke in there somewhere; no, now that's a shame – hass, hass…

Anyway, McCarthy, the only recognised name he'd fought and beaten prior to opposing myself was a certain Courtney Fry the previous summer.

I was confident though.

You have to be really and I knew, we all knew that, deep down, I had to go into the Hydro and win. A loss for me and it would have been a case of where do I go from here.

I wasn't going to become a journeyman, and I certainly wasn't ready to spend the next 12-18 months either waiting for a fight, or fighting journeymen.

I like a challenge, as I've said many times before, and I like there to be something on the line as well, after all, we're in this game to win things surely.

So, here I was, preparing for a trip north o' the border for the Ricky Burns undercard on May 28 2016 (Burns defeated Michele Di Rocco with an eighth round stoppage for the WBA super lightweight whilst there was a win for Tyrone Nurse against Willie Limond for the British at the same weight as Burns, and appearances for fighters like John Ryder, Scott Cardle, Anthony Ogogo, Connor Benn and Charlie Flynn).

As had been the case after Dawson, after Simmons I was promised fights that never materialised, fights on big shows that kept falling through.

During the previous twelve months to the McCarthy fight things were going good personally and I'd become a father three months after the Simmons fights, Kate having given birth to our very own J-Lo, little Joseph-Lewis, so I did have plenty of time at home.

However, this game is all about keeping active and I only had that over intermittent spells throughout my career. During the first eighteen months I had eight fights and was unbeaten; for twenty-odd months, between July 2011 and April 2013, I had six contests and was again unbeaten whilst winning the Northern Area, English and British titles;

all told I had sixteen fights in under five years whereas after I'd beaten Mike Stafford in a British title defence at the Rainton Meadows Arena, I only had six bouts in three years.

I guess situations like that do show how difficult this fight game can be without a big name promoter and television deals by your side; without those then the rest of us fighters and just chasing the scraps really, hoping to get that break.

I did have some pretty decent, top notch sparring opportunities in the year prior to my opposing Tommy McCarthy though with the chance to head over to Latvia and a camp with the then IBF Intercontinental cruiserweight champion, Mairis Briedis (the title had been in two rounds against Danie Venter, Riga, in February 2016 before going on to defeat Marco Huck for the IBO and WBC World cruiserweight titles in April 2017, losing them to Ukrainian powerhouse, Oleksandr Usyk, in January 2018 – Usyk went on to defeat Tony Bellew later in the year).

Going over to Eastern Europe and spending time there, with somebody of that quality and stature in the fight game, certainly instilled further confidence within me, told me that I was certainly capable of handling my own at the level of the cruiserweights.

It was an opportunity that I had to take, you don't pass up chances like that, a once-in-a-lifetime chance and here I was sparring with one of the best the world had to offer (the WBC title has been held by Carlos De Leon 1983-89, Anaclet Wamba 1991-94, Marcelo Fabian Dominguez 1995-97, Juan Carlos Gomez 1998-2001, Krzyzstof Wlodarczyk 2010-13, and more recently, that of Bellew, Brieidis and Usyk).

Doing this therefore gave me a sense, an idea, as to where I was at in my career, or more where I should be at and that I knew, in myself at least, as to what I was capable of.

I was Britain's cruiserweight king and, at that time, I felt I should be looking at rematches with Tony Bellew, that amateur still rankles to this day, and Ovill McKenzie, who'd beaten me for the British and Commonwealth titles, whilst my time were looking at other possibilities; what I got was Svacina, and an eliminator for my old British title against McCarthy.

In facing McCarthy though, it was a tough fight really, in many ways.

I was put on the canvas, hard, got back up, had my jaw broken for a second time, and still, somehow, managed to see the contest out. I think I was actually surprised that I didn't get something from that contest after all that.

Had I won that night in Glasgow I probably would have continued but I wasn't prepared to sit around waiting on things yet again that I knew, deep down, were not going to happen.

I had come back from a broken jaw once before but had to take close to a year out but this time things were completely different and I though, yes, it's time to hang up the gloves and walk away – how much more of this punishment lark can I really take. That and I felt old when I was fighting McCarthy, it wasn't me.

Our Travis had retired himself not that long before I hung up the leather and, don't forget, he'd had a decent run as well adding a fight of the year with Matty Clarkson to his honours list.

Most importantly though, for my health and body, just, they were still intact and I had a young wife and son that I needed to take care of as well.

The way things are now though, here in the north-east, in late 2018, if that was happening what five years ago, heck even two years back in 2016 when I was retiring, things would have been different for me. Opportunities are plenty in 2018, in late 2015, early 2016, there was little happening.

I always managed really good ticket sales and always did my end of the deal.

I'd have loved to have had a lot more shows between 2013 and 2016 as I wouldn't have been as inactive as I'd become and that's what had upset me.

Now though, I prefer the way things are because in those latter stages of my career I didn't know what was happening. Boxing had become something of an inconvenience not only for myself, but for my family, friends, and fans.

. . .

ELDER BROTHER MARK, who's three sons Jack, Mark and Jacob have stepped through the ropes, looked back in thought at his brothers' retirement saying: "We had a feeling that he was going to retire.

"In losing the fights he did, towards the end, they were fights that he should have won but you also have to live the life of a boxer fully, that's what it's all about.

"Now though, he seems really happy since he left boxing and he's gone on and done well for himself."

LOOKING BACK at that night in Scotland, against McCarthy, former promoter Lewis Pendleton said of the occasion: "Jon-Lewis had the best of everything in the build-up to McCarthy, a fantastic training camp.

"When he was in there though he was a shadow of his former self and it was really hard to watch – it took me a long time to get over it and a lot of us feel that, the Jon-Lewis Dickinson who defeated Neil Dawson and Stephen Simmons would have beaten Tommy McCarthy.

"There was a change in him though and he struggled to get his shots off as he used to, it happens though and it was sad to see after all he had done in the sport.

"I'd have loved to have seen him go on and fight for a European title or other major titles but we'd attempted to retire him a few times beforehand, I guess McCarthy was a case of third time lucky in that respect."

SPEAKING of how things are now for the Dickinson household since Jon-Lewis hung up the gloves, wife Kate added: "We know a lot more now where we're at with things and I'd never thought that he'd get seriously injured, or even die when he was in the ring.

"After all that's happened since he retired, with the death of (Scott) Westgarth and those other serious injuries, you just never think that these things could happen to you."

In Ronnie, who'd seen Jon-Lewis, and Travis, progress since they were in their early teens, the Team Dickinson mentor had an idea the timing was right to call it a day.

"Towards the end, with what was happening, you had to have not only the desire, but also a backer," Ronnie continued.

"We didn't want him fighting journeymen, none of us did, and, in the end, it was his decision to leave the sport when he did and we just worked everything around that.

"He's been a successful boxer in his own right and is now, moving forward, a successful businessman and family man."

Cruiserweight Dickinson calls it a day

In March of 2014 Tyneside cruiserweight Jon-Lewis Dickinson, 17-5(5), claimed the Lord Lonsdale belt outright with a tenth round stoppage of challenger Neil Dawson at Newcastle's Metro Radio Arena, a little over two years later and he's hung up his gloves.

Politics have played a big part in his decision to walk away, that and at 30-years-old, he has a wife and young son at home to contend with. He's enjoyed the ride though, twenty years through the amateur and professional ranks say as much.

Having started out under the tutelage of the-then Frank (now Kelly) Maloney with fights in Wigan and Stoke, Dickinson soon became a household name when, within eight fights (and eighteen months) was crowned cruiserweight Prizefighter at York Hall.

"I'm happy and think it's the right time."

"I did what I could and have no regrets; I've the rest of my life to look forward to as life goes on. I've a loving family in wife Kate and our son Joseph-Lewis so it's time to concentrate on them – and my good looks of course."

He does believe he has done things the traditional way though, the right way, and took the correct steps up boxing's ladder.

There's no regrets for the Edmondsley fighter who followed up Prizefighter success in 2010 by winning the Northern Area (2011), English (2012), then the

Lord Lonsdale (British, 2012-14) title outright during a magnificent three-year run, and says that other fighters should follow in his footsteps, and do things the right way – to step up and be counted.

"I'm the first Prizefighter champion from the region and the only fighter here to do things the right way, one title at a time, and enjoyed myself doing it," stated Dickinson.

"Winning the Prizefighter was amazing, a cracking night and I loved it; beating a then undefeated Matty Askin for the English title when I was the underdog; and Simmons (at the Metro Arena for the WBC International) – that was a very special night in front of an unbelievable crowd.

"I only achieved what I have because I went out there and did it – when I beat Dolan (for the Area title), it was on the back of a broken jaw against a tough fighter who was a sizeable name at the time. I did it, so I think they should step up to the plate and take it."

Sponsored long-term by WM Utilities, Dickinson has been trained throughout the amateur and pro ranks by long-time friends and mentors, Ronnie Rowe and Gary Barr, as well as having Martin Nugent Strength & Conditioning keeping him in the best possible shape during his championship run.

For now, it's about family, and enjoying life as a husband and father.

(Dickinson retirement article published in Boxing News magazine, July 2016)

TWELVE

The Family Man

EVEN WHILST I'VE been boxing I've been pretty much working most my life, labouring, doing some serious, hard graft. At times though, boxing may not have been possible without the sponsorship that Christopher Welch and WM Utilities provided, I owe them a lot.

At the end of the day, working every hour which god sends pays the bills, it keeps a roof over your head, clothes and feeds you, so the support and generosity of people has been amazing really.

Since I left the boxing scene, after the loss to McCarthy, life has been pretty good as well. I have a loving wife in Kate, a crazy son on Joseph-Lewis, and a close knit group of friends and family who have been there for a long time.

I somehow even managed to set up my own business, JLD Ground-works & Grab Hire, something a lot of people maybe thought I couldn't, or wouldn't do.

My family life is fantastic and we are loving watching little Joseph-Lewis grow up; he's a character that's for sure, just like his old man so I dread to think what he'll be like when he's older and I do think we all agree on that one.

We've enjoyed some fantastic holidays, together as a family, and some lads' trips and its' much easier now than when I was boxing and

I'm sure the lads boxing will agree. It really did get to the point that I was getting sick of not being able to book, or even having to cancel a holiday, because of changes in fight dates, or not even knowing what was happening with one.

When you're a professional athlete that's the main issue, being unable to plan family time, holidays, even having nights out and meals because of training regime and strict diets. I was always in training camps but, towards the end, fight dates weren't as forthcoming, which hampered things more.

JON-LEWIS' mother, Jacqui Dickinson, along with the rest of the family, are understandably proud of what has become of him, and of Travis, a final word of hers being: "Things are going really well for him since he retired.

"He's a very well respected, loving person, a good worker and very reliable which he'll continue to be, I'm sure of it."

Hass! Hass!

Appendix I

STATISTICS

Born – 3 May 1986; Edmondsley, County Durham

Third of four children, siblings are Mark, Leanne and Travis Dickinson

Married – 9 August 2014, Kate Williams; one son, Joseph-Lewis Dickinson, 6 August 2015

HONOURS

Junior ABA champion – 2003, 2004

NABC champion – 2003

Four Nations Gold – 2003

Senior ABA finalist (heavyweight) - 2005

Senior ABA champion (cruiserweight) – 2007

Tyneside Senior Boxer of the Year – 2007

Prizefighter champion (cruiserweight) – 2010

Northern Area champion (cruiserweight) – 2011

English champion (cruiserweight) – 2012

British champion (cruiserweight) -2012

British champion (outright, cruiserweight) – 2014

WBC International Silver champion (cruiserweight) - 2015

Maurice Cullen Memorial Trophy – 2017

BBB Lifetime Achievement – 2018

PROFESSIONAL RECORD - 17-5(6)
(Opponents records, in brackets, are that prior to facing Jon-Lewis Dickinson; scores are with Dickinson first)

7 November 2008 Robin Park Centre, Wigan
    Paul Bonson (20-102-8) Won PTS4 (40-36)
    Referee – Steve Gray
    Professional debut for Jon-Lewis Dickinson

23 January 2009 Fenton Manor Sports Complex, Stoke
    John Anthony (6-9) Won PTS4 (40-36)
    Referee – Robert Chalmers

2 May 2009 Crowtree Leisure Centre, Sunderland
    Nick Okoth (8-21-5) Won PTS4 (39-38)
    Referee – Graeme Williams

10 July 2009 Seaburn Centre, Sunderland
    Hastings Rasani (19-41-3) Won PTS4 (40-37)
    Referee – Graeme Williams

16 October 2009 Seaburn Centre, Sunderland
    Martyn Grainger (3-1) Won PTS 4 (40-37)
    Referee – Graeme Williams

30 April 2010 York Hall, Bethnal Green
    Nick Okoth (9-27-5) Won KO3
    Referee – Richard James Davies
    Prizefighter quarter-final

30 April 2010 York Hall, Bethnal Green
    Mark Krence (25-7) Won RTD1
    Referee – Victor Loughlin

Prizefighter semi-final

30 April 2010 York Hall, Bethnal Green
    Leon Williams (4-1) Won SD3 (28-27, 28-29, 29-28)
    Referee – Phil Edwards
    Prizefighter final

23 July 2010 Rainton Meadows Arena, Houghton-le-Spring
    Tyrone Wright (8-4-2) Lost TKO3
    Referee – Andrew Wright

11 September 2010 Rainton Meadows Arena, Houghton-le-Spring
    Richard Turba (4-2-1) Lost RTD3
    Referee – Mark Curry

3 July 2011 Stadium of Light, Sunderland
    David Dolan (14-3-1) Won PTS10 (97-94)
    Referee – Mark Curry
    Northern Area cruiserweight championship contest

25 February 2012 Exhibition Centre, Aberdeen
    Chris Burton (15-1) Won TKO2
    Referee – Victor Loughlin

21 April 2012 Oldham Sports Centre, Oldham
    Matty Askin (13-0) Won UD10 (98-93, 97-93, 97-93)
    Referee – Phil Edwards
    English cruiserweight championship contest
    13 October 2012 Echo Arena, Liverpool
    Shane McPhilbin (8-3) Won UD12 (118-110, 117-111, 118-110)
    Referee – Steve Gray
    British cruiserweight championship contest

15 February 2013 Rainton Meadows Arena, Houghton-le-Spring
    David Dolan (16-4-1) Won UD12 (118-111, 118-111, 117-112)

Referee – Phil Edwards
British cruiserweight championship contest

19 April 2013 Rainton Meadows Arena, Houghton-le-Spring
   Mike Stafford (11-1) Won UD12 (118-112, 117-112, 115-113)
   Referee - Victor Loughlin
   British cruiserweight championship contest

29 March 2014 Metro Radio Arena, Newcastle
   Neil Dawson (12-2) Won TKO10
   Referee – Phil Edwards
   British Cruiserweight championship (outright) contest

7 June 2014 Metro Radio Arena, Newcastle
   Ovill McKenzie (22-12) Lost TKO2
   Referee – Victor Loughlin
   British & Commonwealth cruiserweight championship contest

29 November 2014 Gateshead Leisure Centre, Gateshead
   Courtney Fry (18-6) Lost PTS10 (94-95)
   Referee – Andrew Wright
   4 April 2015 Metro Radio Arena, Newcastle
   Stephen Simmons (11-0) Won TKO8
   Referee – Ian John Lewis
   WBC International Silver cruiserweight championship contest

26 March 2016 Gateshead Leisure Centre, Gateshead
   Jiri Svacina (12-18) Won PTS6 (60-54)
   Referee – Andrew Wright

28 May 2016 SSE Hydro, Scotland
   Tommy McCarthy (8-0) Lost UD10 (97-92, 97-92, 98-91)
   Referee - Michael Alexander
   British cruiserweight championship eliminator contest

Jon-Lewis Dickinson fought 137 rounds of professional boxing and face three undefeated opponents in Matty Askin, Stephen Simmons and Tommy McCarthy.

Of his 22 contests, 13 came at home of which he won nine, and nine were away in which he won eight times.

Appendix II

CONTRIBUTIONS

The following pages sees (additional) contributions from those who knew Jon-Lewis Dickinson the boxer (primarily) with additional words from his family, and from the author....

Kellie Maloney (formerly Frank Maloney) – former promoter and manager

I've always believed that, If I could have moulded the qualities of Jon-Lewis and Travis Dickinson, I'd have had another world champion on my books.

Travis was a good, nasty fighter, box office material, whilst Jon-Lewis was your classical fighter, someone the boxing purists would want, and I was in the middle of them both.

You'd have the ultimate fighting machine if you could combine those two and that's the best compliment that I could pay them both.

David Venn – Northern Area Council

Jon was a credit to the sport both in and, especially out of, the ring. He came back from a horrible injury - the badly broken jaw; he won a Lonsdale Belt outright - even more difficult nowadays since it became necessary to win four fights for the same title (I'm pretty sure he was the first from our Area to achieve this - all his predecessors like Maurice Cullen, Billy Hardy George Feeney etc only needed 3 wins) - and he got out when his high standards started to slide.

He was awarded the Maurice Cullen trophy and supported Ronnie Rowe when he received the same trophy; he has behaved himself in a manner we would all hope - sometimes forlornly - our sporting heroes behave, and I cannot speak highly enough of him.

I've told him that, as an Area, we'd support any application he might care to make as a trainer and, if he chooses not to go down that route, there would be an immediate role for him with the Area Council.

John Gibson – Sports Writer NCJ Media

Jon-Lewis was a standard bearer for North East boxing, a great champion from a family of true boxing tradition, and a belting bloke into the bargain.

After a lull following the triple impact of superstars like Glenn McCrory, Billy Hardy, and John Davison who I followed in all their top fights along came Dickinson to put us back on the map and open the door for others to follow.

The man won a Lonsdale Belt outright and under the shrewd guidance of Ronnie Rowe, both as an amateur at Birtley and a pro, he achieved so much from Prizefighter to Area champ, English, and finally British cruiser dominance.

I count Jon-Lewis as a friend and I'm privileged to call him that.

Craig Johns – Sports Writer NCJ Media

In my role as boxing reporter for the Chronicle, Journal and Sunday Sun I've had the pleasure of being ringside for so many great fight nights, and in doing so meeting so many great names in the sport - both nationally known and regionally too.

I can honestly say that Jon Lewis would be up there among the most talented.

Rewind to April 2010 and I hadn't even started university at that point. I'd always been a huge fan of boxing stretching back to staying up late to watch Prince Naseem and Joe Calzaghe fights, and I remember tuning in to that month's Prizefighter on Sky Sports which featured cruiserweights.

I might be a Sunderland lad myself, but seeing Jon, a Geordie, in the competition made me instantly root for him without any prior knowledge to who he was. That was the first time I watched Jon box and you may remember he was brilliant that evening, winning the competition outright to set off on what would become a remarkable career.

Fast forward 15 months and I had started my university degree in sports journalism and as part of that had started reporting on local boxing. Jon was to fight Sunderland cruiserweight David Dolan at the Stadium of Light for the Northern Area title on what has now become an annual show from promoter and manager Phil Jeffries called the Summer Rumble.

I'd been invited along to the press conference and that would be the first time I would meet Jon. Here I was, a young budding journalist, about to meet who to me at the time was a pretty big deal, having watched him win Prizefighter just over a year ago. I was s******** myself, to be quite truthful!

I needn't have been.

I came to learn over the years that there are few nicer people than the North East boxing community, and Jon certainly fights right into that family ethos we have up here.

Jon would win that fight against Dolan and would go on to win the British title and defend it three times (one a rematch against Dolan), meaning he owns that famous Lord Lonsdale belt outright.

I was fortunate to be there ringside for the most of Jon's big nights and it was always a pleasure to watch him box.

While he might not always have been the most exciting fighter to watch, technically he was superb.

If I was to pick out one stand-out moment for me personally, it would have to be the Stephen Simmons victory.

By this point in 2015 I knew Jon well and had grew to really like him on a personal level as well as professional. He'd had a bad run going into that huge Simmons fight at the Metro Radio Arena on the under card of a Matchroom show that featured Anthony Joshua. He'd lost his last two against Ovill McKenzie and Courtney Fry and many felt that his career rested on a tough fight against a highly touted Scot in Simmons.

Dickinson was phenomenal that night though.

Not only was he in bad form, he'd also seen his brother Travis upset earlier in the night in a fight against a Spaniard who he should have been dealing with comfortably. I can't imagine the place Jon would have been in mentally heading to the ring that night.

But in testament to the talent that he was, Jon broke down Simmons and stopped him in the eighth.

I'll never forget the eruption from the fans as the referee waved it off and Jon sank to his knees in delight. The hairs on my arms certainly stood to attention.

In conclusion, I think the biggest compliment I can give Jon is that, not only was he such a fantastic boxer, but he's an absolute gentleman outside the ring too. A kind-hearted, funny, charming and charismatic individual who deserves to be remembered as one of Newcastle's finest ever pugilists.

Roy Kelly – Boxing News, Punchlines, Hartlepool Life

Just what is it about the North-East of England and cruiserweight? Answers on a postcard please!

Seriously, why is our incredible fighting region synonymous with the fellas who go through, blood, sweat and tears to tip the scales at 200lbs?

First, there was Stewart Lithgo, a heavyweight from Hartlepool, who travelled 12,000 miles to Australia in 1985 to knock-out home favourite Steve Aczel to become the Commonwealth's first cruiserweight title winner.

It was a belt Annfield Plain's most famous sporting son, Glenn McCrory would go on to lift.

Then, most famously, 'Gentleman Glenn' did even better by winning the IBF world title on a famous night in Stanley in 1989 when he outpointed Patrick Lumumba.

Another North-East heavy, Hartlepool's Dave Garside made an

unsuccessful bid to be Commonwealth and British cruiserweight champ, as did a man he managed, David Dolan, the Sunderland fighter missing out on three occasions.

Which brings me, finally to the subject of this book, Jon Lewis Dickinson, the man who brought down the curtain on David's career.

Of course, McCrory is the daddy of all our region's cruisers, for so long he remained the North-East's only leading world sanctioning body champ, but in terms of longevity in the 200lb division, certainly in the 21st century, you could not look further than Jon Lewis.

What a fighter, what a man.

That Dickinson could fight was never a surprise given he was a product on that famous Birtley production line masterminded by Ronnie Rowe.

Jon Lewis took to the pro game like the proverbial duck to water when he turned over in 2008 but it was his five years at the top of the cruiserweight division which sets him on a pedestal.

My job in his time at the summit was with the Hartlepool Mail, which meant on three occasions Jon Lewis was the opposition to 'my' fighter.

Each time Dickinson triumphed and triumphed well.

Phil Jeffries staged Dickinson v Dolan for the Northern Area title at the 2011 Summer Rumble, Jon Lewis winning a cracker 97-94 on the card of Mark Curry.

Seven months later, I made a near 600-mile round trip to Aberdeen for just five minutes of 'action' as Dickinson stopped Chris Burton in what had been set as a title defence. Thanks for that Jon Lewis!

That was the signal that Jon Lewis meant business and he became English champ with a great win over Matty Askin, following that up by becoming British champion with a landslide success over Shane McPhilbin.

That set up Dickinson-Dolan 2 at the Rainton Meadows Arena.

Almost a year to the day that he made my journey to Aberdeen a fruitless one, he repeated the trick against the 2002 Commonwealth Games gold medallist. At least Houghton was on my doorstep this time!

Dickinson was in supreme form, a man at the height off his powers and he clinched another unanimous decision.

Two further defences followed, both on home soil, including a stoppage win at the Metro Radio Arena which brought the house down. It was a privilege to be ringside for that one.

To be honest, it was a pleasure to be ringside every time to watch Jon Lewis.

Yes, as mentioned, boy could he fight, but there was more to him than that. He was one of life's nice guys, still is in fact.

Modest, down-to-earth, polite, he never got involved in any shenanigans before the big occasions, he made weight, he shook hands, he fought, invariably won and shook hands again.

Fans will all have their favourite Jon Lewis Dickinson fights, his Prizefighter triumph, his stoppage victory over unbeaten Stephen Simmons for the World Boxing Council International Silver Cruiserweight title, what a mouthful, on the night Anthony Joshua came to Toon.

This observer will recall those five years at the top of the 200lb division between 2011-15 as his greatest and he full deserves to be the subject of this work by Peter Mann.

What a fighter, what a man.

British Boxing Blog (Andrew Newton and Steven Lowe)

Outside of the ring, Jon has been nothing but an absolute gentleman to us both. He didn't have to speak to us but agreed to an interview (before what was his last fight), which just shows what sort of a man he is. He also offered us great encouragement and support at a time when he barely knew us.

Inside the ring, he has been a true pioneer for North East boxing. His accomplishments are superb and he can rightly be proud of what he has achieved. There are many great boxers who never managed to win the Lonsdale title outright and his Prizefighter win will always be one of my favourite memories of the sport.

Due to these factors, it was a very easy decision to award Jon the Lifetime Achievement Award at our North East Boxing Awards ceremony. Jon thoroughly deserves the recognition and has certainly earned his retirement. He certainly doesn't need my encouragement to enjoy it!

Phil Jeffries Wearside Promoter/Manager

I have promoted Jon-Lewis for years on and off and he was always a gentleman.

He was very tough and had great fights including winning the derby, against David Dolan; he and his brother Travis winning the Prizefighter helped north-east boxing a lot and he was always a pleasure to work with and promote.

Steve Wraith – Tyneside Promoter/Manager

Jon-Lewis Dickinson is a credit to the sport of boxing in the North East.

He was dedicated to the sport and during what can only be described as the barren years of North-East boxing he was a shining light and gave fight fans something to shout about with his performances always entertaining.

He is also a great lad who is great fun to be around but I'm not so sure about his singing.

He can sit back in his armchair in years to come and say he gave his all to the sport and if anybody deserved to retain a Lonsdale belt then he did.

Any youngster wanting to make the jump into the pro game should seek him out for a chat, there is nothing he doesn't know.

Ron Kearney – Referee

Although I don't know him that well, when we have spoken he's always been a gentleman. He's very knowledgeable about boxing and his record doesn't lie, amateur or professional.

One thing I'd say is John is a great example of the gentleman's sport; always humble and very respectful every time I've seen him.

Graeme Williams - Referee

I refereed Jon-Lewis three times early on in his career when he was starting out. I remember he turned over about the same time as his brother Travis and, at the time, I think it's fair to say Travis was catching people's eye more than Jon-Lewis as he was a more aggressive fighter.

I always liked the look of Jon-Lewis more though and he was a really solid box-fighter, a good rounded professional who had a really good career. I think it's fair to say he was one of the better fighters to come out of the North East, and I think will be remembered as a very good, honest pro who had a career he can be proud of.

Mark White – Fighting Chance Promotions boxer

Jon-Lewis is a cracking character to have in the gym, full of experience & knowledge.

It was good training alongside him as it just made you want to push yourself to get to that that level in the game.

He's full of great banter also!

Andrew Buchanan – Fighting Chance Promotions (former Birtley ABC)

I was halfway through my first retirement (2005-13) when Jon-Lewis made his pro debut but knew of him before that, we both originate from Birtley.

I won my titles and England vests at Birtley, which was even before Gary (Barr) started there so yeah, I had my fight education and a connection with them and Ronnie Rowe.

When Fighting Chance started up it was logical for me to go back there, with them, with Jon-Lewis, Travis and Craig Dixon.

I always kept in touch with what the news was out of Birtley and Jon-Lewis massively achieved in the amateurs, then the professionals also. I watched him win the British outright at the Arena and was looking forward to meeting him when I joined Fighting Chance.

We did a few training sessions together and was the consummate professional, tech sparring was fantastic and he was a big character, a really good and experienced team-mate; he always kept people in good spirits and had that presence about him, was always going to stand out for his professionalism.

His achievements, amateur and professional, are amazing and that commands respect so he;s highly thought of and rightly so, he's done everybody proud.

Kyle Redfearn – Fighting Chance Promotions

I'd done a few bits of sparring with him before I joined up with him and the lads at Fighting Chance and he's a bit of a legend really, what with all he's done in the sport.

Jon-Lewis has always been a hard worker, very disciplined when in a training camp and when I got in a ring with him he had to take it easy on me so it was touch sparring. I'm a few stones lighter, probably more now, than him and he was a big lump of a lad but lean with it.

For me, in my career, if I can achieve even half of what he did then I'd be happy. He's the benchmark for a lot of us and my own goal is to achieve that British title myself.

Jone TK Volau Taukeinikoro – Fighting Chance Promotions

I've sparred loads of round with that bloke and he's a proper genuine man.

When I turned professional he brought himself down to my level so I wasn't outclassed or belittled or anything, he made me realize that, as a heavyweight, it's never too late, that and everybody looks up to him, we all did in the gym.

The Fighting Chance gym was always buzzing every time he came in and I learnt a lot from him, the different levels when you're in the ring; he taught me the best times in which to move, when to up the tempo, to slow down, everything.

You realize quickly that you have to keep busy and work hard with him though as he has a tremendous jab as well as a nice, tight guard; he's one of the top operators and all fighters should strive to achieve what he has done – he's definitely a benchmark.

I'm happy for Jon-Lewis and all he has done, he's accomplished a lot, personally and professionally, and has a beautiful family, a wonderful wife and son, and a good business.

China Clarke – former amateur opponent and sparring partner, professional boxer turned triathlete

I was very raw when I boxed Jon-Lewis in the amateurs. I'd first walked into a gym when I was 17 and had a few fights before jumping out for about a year.

I got bumped up a few levels when facing him though, the lesser skilled fighter was easy enough but he was more experienced and, although he was a kid himself he was huge, but lean, and he carried it well. He was the first, very good boxer I'd faced so I couldn't get away with things I had done and I knew that I was beaten, not out of fear though, before I got into the ring.

I talked myself out of it and he was one of only a few losses I had before turning professional. I was meant to make my debut the day Scott Quigg made his 9 April 2007) and he took my place as I was out injured with a fractured hand, something I'd suffered a few times.

There was never any talk of Jon-Lewis and I facing each other in the pros though but we did spar each other on a number of occasions.

With Jon-Lewis, and Travis, even when they came to Leeds, they were really pleasant and respectful – we had some pretty good times together. Facing him though, it showed me how much I'd come on and we had pretty equal styles to each other so he didn't fully have my number though.

David Dolan – opponent for English, and British title

I was coming back from an injury but felt sharp having torn my peck in the second round against Terry Dunstan and was out of action.

Preparing for Jon-Lewis has been great because he is more conventional than some of the lads I have had to train for, like Norton, who grabs and holds.

I had sparred with Jon-Lewis five or six times, he is a good boxer and I'm expecting it be close in the early stages but I'm the more rounded boxer and I'm sure I will prevail.

Getting past Jon-Lewis would have put me back into contention and I didn't really care who the British champion was, I'd fight anyone but it would have been nice to be Norton. I gave it everything when I boxed him last time and I pressured him nonstop.

(Dolan quoted in the fight programme for the 2011 Summer Rumble at the Stadium of Light)

Stephen Simmons – opponent for WBC International Silver

Jon-Lewis Dickinson is alright at what he does but I found him very one paced and I didn't think he'd be able to bring the same work rate that I bring to the table.

He has my utmost respect and I had a job to do (at Geordie Roar) which is what I was looking forward to doing.

His strength is probably his movement and his weakness his work rate and felt he wasn't able to take a decent shot, as we'd seen in his previous couple of fights.

I expected him to be on the back foot and didn't expect him to try and fight me, I expected him to try and box me, surprise us but I doubted it.

I thought his tactics were to box me on the outside and try and win the fight from there without getting involved.

A loss wouldn't have put him back too much because of the level of opponent he was fighting, he was fighting me, not just anybody.

A loss to me wouldn't have left him with limited options because he could build himself back up and I was up-and-coming and looking to take out everybody who was in my way.

(Simmons quoted in the fight programme for the 2015 Geordie Roar at the Metro Radio Arena)

Gary Barr – friend and former coach

Jon-Lewis was very respectful of myself and Ronnie professionally and we've always been great mates.

As for stories, there's none that we can put in a book I can tell you but, when you look at what's he's achieved, with the setbacks that he's had, then he was always chomping at the bit and I'm so proud of him and who he is.

Martin Nugent – former strength & conditioning coach (Martin Nugent Elite Performance)

I started working with both Dickinson's when Jon-Lewis was in his build-up to the English title (against Matty Askin) having across Jon-Lewis and his team through our respective connections with Gateshead College.

Jon-Lewis and Travis were the first professionals I had on my strength programmes and he was great to have around the place; everybody bought into him and what he was about.

Strength & Conditioning wasn't really used so much back then but Jon-Lewis was very proactive and open to what I could bring to the table because I'm not a coach, I'm more of a scientist and it was rare that boxing coaches would allow others to work with their athletes.

Jon-Lewis wanted to look at how he could be better, improve himself as an athlete and, because of Ronnie, we were able to achieve. We looked at what Jon-Lewis could improve upon so that' what we did prior to each of his fights having sat and put specific plans in place.

I fast became an integral part of his week from then on and generally we would be doing three-four sessions per week in accordance to Ronnie's instruction; it was a case of making him more robust as both he, and Travis, had niggly back issues (due to height) and because of what we did he became stronger, more powerful.

He really bought into what I was doing and everything had to be right but he could see the differences we were making. I had the tools he needed and what he got from it was down to him. He was so switched on when he was in camp, always wanting to learn, very reliable and was an absolute pleasure to be around.

He's not just an athlete, he's a friend, a great character to have around and always showed interest.

Steven White – former Fighting Chance photographer

Getting to cover Jon-Lewis' fights was awesome and getting access people can only dream of. It was always a pleasure spending time with Jon during camps capturing the images.

Spending time amongst Jon-Lewis, Ronnie Rowe and the lads was always a highlight of mine.

Christopher Welch – sponsor, owner of WM Utilities

I met him around the time he won the Prizefighter title, he'd come into the local a few days after winning that. It would be about a year or two later that he began to work for me and I'd wanted to get involved with both of the Dickinson's if I'm honest.

It was something that I wanted to do and I got more pleasure than anything else; seeing my company name on their ring gear, on national television, seeing that everywhere – it was certainly more of a personal satisfaction than professional for me.

I've been everywhere watching him fight; Aberdeen, Liverpool, Oldham. Going to Aberdeen, now that was a good night, there was a lot of us went up there for that one.

He's one of those lads though that would do anything for you and we don't go that long a time without seeing each other; he's just a proper, down to earth bloke.

From the Family

Jon Dickinson – Jon-Lewis and Travis Dickinson's father

Those two boys, Jon-Lewis and Travis, they'd do the most damage to each other when they were in the ring and sparring with each other.

Right back at the beginning though, after his early fights in the amateurs – we're so very proud of you son.

Mark Dickinson - elder sibling of the Dickinson's

I'd already grown up, left home, got married and had my first child (Jack) when Jon-Lewis had his first amateur fight and I went to all his fights.

He and our Leanne always fought though, I guess it's because they were so close in age, that and Leanne was always daddy's girl; him and Travis though, they had some scraps as well that's for sure.

I remember him fighting Tony Hill in the schoolboys' finals which was a great fight and was when he came good as a boxer; he was Graeme Rutherford's first boys' club champion, and then there was the fight with DeGale as well.

However, I think it was difficult for him at his weight with the differentiations that was then, it's all different now so his turning professional was probably the right time for him, and it was just difficult with the lack of opportunities in the region.

I am really proud though, watching him win all those titles, made me wish that I'd gone into boxing myself so I'm pleased my own boys followed in Jon-Lewis and Travis' footsteps – Jack, Mark and Jacob having donned gloves.

I'm proud of him and not many here in the region have won the Lonsdale belt outright, it's a difficult thing to achieve, he also put in a great performance for the English against Matty Askin which for me was his best performance as a boxer and was a fight he wasn't supposed to win, Matty being a heavy favourite.

Leanne Dickinson - Jon-Lewis and Travis Dickinson's sister

There's never been a dull moment with any of my brothers really but I know that they've always got my back.

Jon-Lewis though, he's an absolute gentleman and you really can rely on his a hundred percent.

He's worked so hard for all that he's got, and done, in his life, but I'm still the boss of him though and he's mellowed a lot over the years and grown up massively. I'd put my life in his hands, he means that much to me.

Kate Dickinson – long-suffering wife and mother to Joseph-Lewis

He's very dramatic, he's always having a mariah and he likes a good bit of gossip, always wanting to know what everyone's craic is.

His favourite excuse for not doing any DIY and other stuff around the house was "I need to rest, resting is more important than the training."

From the Author – Peter Mann
(www.insidemannmedia.wordpress.com)

I've known Jon-Lewis for quite a few years now, even before I worked with him in a media capacity in the boxing; we used to both go and watch the same Sunday League football matches which my mother and sisters volunteered at.

When I first started boxing journalism, in early 2012, Jon-Lewis was one of the first interviews I conducted, he and Brian Rose being published on American combat sports website, Real Combat Media, who I was with during that year.

Since that day, at Birtley ABC, we kept in touch and I began working more closely with him, his brother Travis, and Craig Dixon, running their respective social media outlets. Then, with the formation of Fighting Chance Promotions, it became a logical transition, my being their first press officer (ably followed by Nathan Orr and Jake Swinburn) and merged the three fighters' socials to launch the FCP presence.

I've seen Jon-Lewis fight on numerous occasions during his professional career with a personal highlight being the victory over Stephen Simmons at the Arena, that was some night that's for sure and, knowing what victory meant for Jon-Lewis, I recall an outpouring of emotion from not only myself, but others, at ringside.

Because of my connection to Jon-Lewis I've become friends with several connected to him, lads such as Matty Askin and China Clarke, both of whom I've done regular media for as well over the years.

My talking about Jon-Lewis and Travis wouldn't really be complete without those two stories, their nicknaming me, and that night out.

So, for the record, it was Jon-Lewis and Travis who named me 'G-String,' it's the first, and last, time I put a request on social media – I only asked for peoples thoughts on a possible pen-name for me, as others sometimes do; never again as they were the first to pipe up with that which has stuck ever since.

Then there's that night in Chester-le-Street, well I'm saying a night, it technically wasn't, or was, depending how you look at it. I'd actually been invited to one of Martyn Devlin's annual awards dinners in Newcastle that the Dickinson's were at – it was a pretty decent function as well. The brothers had offered me a lift home but on the condition I went for a drink with them.

Now, people who know me, know I'm not a big drinker, my eldest sister will agree to that one; however, going for a drink with this lot meant keeping up with them as well and that was never going to happen as they can't half put them away. I managed five pints in about an hour before bailing so lads and lasses, if you're ever invited out with them, know what you're in for.

As for this, 'Cruising to Glory,' it had been in the pipeline long before we actually started it. I'd approached Jon-Lewis during the latter stages of his pro career and, although there was interest, we felt it was best to leave it until a later date. I continued doing occasional press for him and, after he retired, I would go on to release two music books in early 2018.

Shortly before that we'd met up and discussed my ghosting his life story so, after the other two were published, through Britain's Next Bestseller, this was brought back to the fore, and it's been fun doing it, catching up with people I'd not spoken to for a while, and making a few new friends along the way.

And I can vouch for everything that everybody says that is good about Jon-Lewis, not that anyone has said anything bad...

About the Author

Peter is a freelance journalist and author based in Northern England.

Born and raised in the pit mining village of Esh Winning, County Durham, he is the eldest of four, brother Michael and sisters Victoria and Elizabeth.

Always having a passion for literature and the arts Peter took to writing after the unexpected death of his brother in 2002, picking up the pen the following year in order to stave off depression.

Initially his journalistic background began in the local non-league football scene, somewhere he has always has found comfort, and basically rose from there.

In 2008 he returned to higher education studying Psychology and Sociology at Gateshead College and it was whilst there he met his mentor and friend, Amanda McQueen.

From there Peter studied a BSc Honours in Sport & Exercise Psychology at Teesside University, graduating in 2012, and has studied the Diploma in Journalism at Darlington College.

A regular contributor to a number of newspapers, magazines and websites producing content on sport, and music, interviewing some of the biggest names in their respective fields.

Peter released his first two books, The Interviews – Vol I: Music, and The Trip of a Lifetime, at the start of 2018 published by Britain's Next Bestseller.

Cruising to Glory is his third book.

You can contact him via email petermann78@homail.com or visit his website www.insidemann.wordpress.com

Images by Steven White